MY BELGIUM

www.swisstravelcenter.ch

THE 10 REGIONS OF BELGIUM

West-Vlaanderen

Oost-Vlaanderen

Antwerpen

Limburg

Vlaams-Brabant

Bruxelles/Brussel

Brabant-Wallon

Hainaut

Liège

Namur

Luxembourg

content

The 10 regions of Belgium 2

Brussels. . . . . 5 – 17

Brabant: Flemish Brabant and Walloon Brabant. . . . . 19 – 35

Liège . . . . 37 – 47

Luxembourg . . . . 49 – 59

Namur. . . . . 61 – 73

Hainaut . . . . 75 – 89

West Flanders. . . . . 91 – 109

East Flanders . . . . 111 – 129

Antwerpen . . . . 131 – 153

Limburg . . . . 155 – 167

English – Captions . . . . 168 – 169

Français – Légende . . . . 170 – 171

Nederlands – Legende. . . . . 172 – 173

Deutsch - Bildlegenden . . . . 174 – 175

Español – Leyendas . . . . 176 – 177

Italiano – Didascalie delle immagini . . . . 178 – 179

Português – Legendas . . . . 180 – 181

Русский – Пояснения . . . . 182 – 183

Polski – Legendy do zdjęć . . . . 184 – 185

Türkçe – Fotoğraf Açıklamaları . . . . 186 – 187

日本語 — 説明 . . . . 188 – 189

中文—图释 . . . . 190 – 191

Picture record - Impressum 192

Brussels

BRUXELLES/BRUSSEL

BRUSSELS - MANNEKEN PIS

cinquantenaire

THE MAROLLES

STREET MUSICIANS

EUROSTAR - HIGH SPEED TRAIN

zinneke parade   musical instrument museum   13

14   WAFFLES

TOONE THEATER

COMIC STRIP TRAIL

ST. MICHAEL AND ST. GUDULA

DIEST

meise - national botanic garden

PHILIPPE LEJEUNE

SUGAR MUSEUM TIENEN

WATERLOO - memorial DaY

THE HErGé MUSEUM - LOUVAIN-LA-NEUVE

LIÈGE

MUSEUM OF WALLOON LIFE

THE PRINCIPAUTAIRES

ST. PAUL - LIÈGE

15TH OF AUGUST FESTIVAL

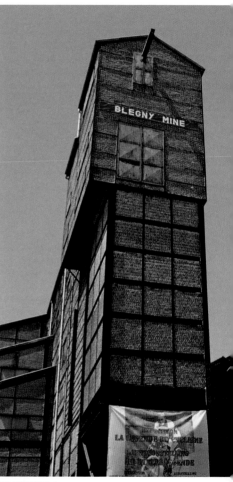

42 LA BATTE - LIÈGE

BLEGNY

Gaufre au Sucre
avec de la
Cannelle
1,30€

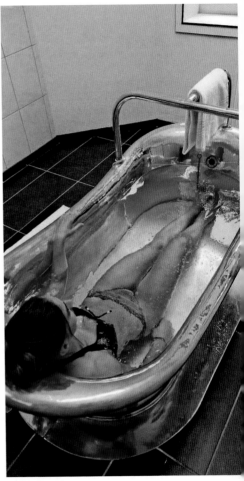

SPa

LUXEMBOURG

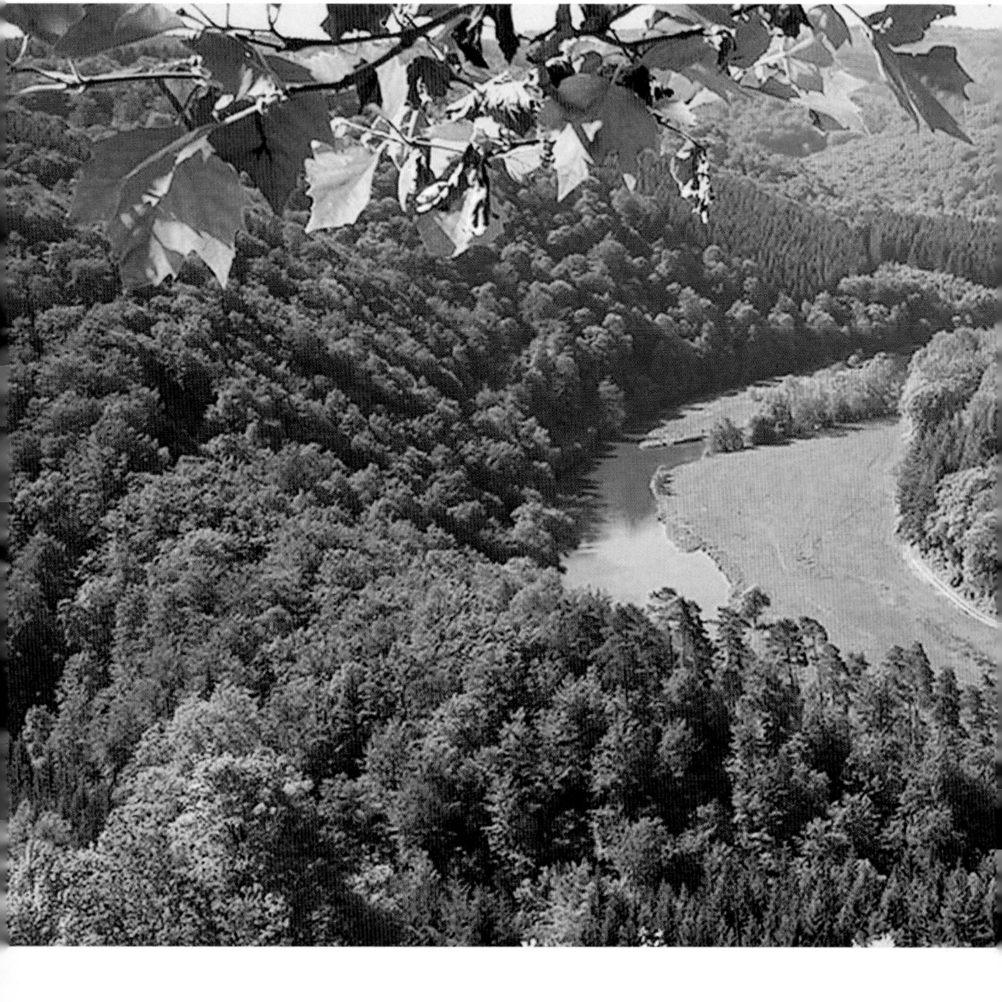

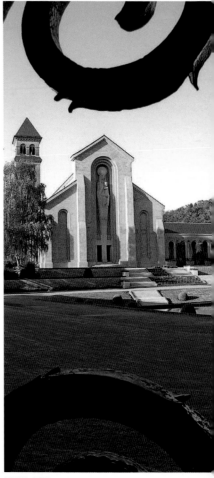

orval

BOUILLON CASTLE

l'ancienne
16€/Kg

GAME SPECIALITY

Gembloux
Grand-Leez
Éghezée
Leuze
Bierwart
Sombreffe
Namur/Namen
Gelbressée
Jemeppe
63 – 65
Nameche
Andenne
Floreffe
70
Bernard
Ohey
Wépion
Profondeville
Assesse
Fosses-l.-V.
Annevoie
Havelange
Méan
Mettet
71
Spontin
Emptinne
Baillon-ville
Yvoir
61
Maredsous
Dinant
Ciney
Florennes
69 70
Achêne
Walcourt
Rosée
Onhaye
Hogne
Hastière-Lavaux
72
Celles
Philippeville
Merlemont
Ciergnon
Cerfontaine
Doische
67
Rochefort
Culot
Mariem-bourg
Beauraing
Han-s-Lesse
Vierves-s-Viroin
68
73
Couvin
Oignies
Willerzie
Brûly
Gedinne
Bièvre
Paliseul
67
Vresse

festival of wallonia - namur

near vresse

brewery st-remy

67

HaN-SUr-LeSSe

RaPe FieLD

THE BAYARD ROCK

STRAWBERRIES OF WÉPION

Warneton

Mouscron

Celles

Pays des Collines

(87)

Lahamaide

Lessines

Pecq

Clipet

Isières

Enghien

Hoves

Quartes

Leuze

Ath

Ghislenghien

Graty

Braine-le-Comte

(77) (78)

Tournai

Chièvres

(84)

Brugelette

Lens

Soignies

Bury

(80) Beloeil

Jurbise

Le Rœulx

(86) Seneffe

Basècles

Péruwelz

Baudour

Manage

Mellet

Fleurus

Ville-Pommerœul

Grand Hornu

Ghlin

Mons/Bergen

(78) (75)

La Louvière

(85)

Boussu

(84)

(81) — (83)

Strépy-Thieu

Binche

Charleroi

Châtelet

Quiévrain

Frameries

Givry

(79)

Anderlues

(87)

Dour

Estinnes

Gougnies

Erquelinnes

Thuin

Gozée

Gerpinnes

Thuillies

Beaumont

Boussu-lez-Walcourt

(89)

Rance

Chimay

Macon

(88)

Bailleux

Macquenoise

Rièzes

BELFRY TOWER OF TOURNAI   STRÉPY-THIEU BOAT LIFT

84 BRUGELETTE

GRAND HORNU

LAND OF THE HILLS

marcinelle

canals in Brugge

DAMME

JAMES ENSOR HOUSE

OOSTENDE – GALERIES LÉOPOLD II

FLEMISH GREY SHRIMPS

Pier in Blankenberge

HERE ARE RECORDED NAMES
OF OFFICERS AND MEN WHO FELL
IN YPRES SALIENT BUT TO WHOM
THE FORTUNE OF WAR DENIED
THE KNOWN AND HONOURED BURIAL
GIVEN TO THEIR COMRADES
IN DEATH

Van Eyck 1432

GRAVENSTEEN - CASTLE OF THE COUNTS

CUBERDONS 119

mattentaarten of Geraardsbergen

CRVV - centre "tour of flanders"

CASTLE OF OOIDONK - DEINZE

antwerpen

Essen
Kalmthoutse Heide
142
Kapellen
Ekeren
Antwerpen/Anvers
131 – 141
Mortsel
Kontich
Niel
151
Bornem
Willebroek
143
144 145
Mechelen
Duffel
Putte
Lier
148 149
Nijlen
Berlaar
Heist o/d Berg
Achterbroek
Brasschaat
Westmalle
Zoersel
Brecht
Wuustwezel
Meerle
Baarle-Hertog (B)
Hoogstraten
Merksplas
Rijkevorsel
Vosselaar
Turnhout
Ravels
Arendonk
Postel
147
Dessel
Mol
153
Balen
Olmen
Geel
Westerlo
Veerle
Herselt
Morkhoven
Herentals
Zandhoven
Lille
Tielen
Lichtaart
152
146
Kasterlee

132
132

GROENPLAATS

mas - museum on the river

KALMTHOUTSE HEIDE

FILET D'ANVERS - SPECIALITY

LIMBURG

NATIONAL PARK HOGE KEMPEN

HASSELT BY NIGHT

sausage specialties

CAPTIONS MY BELGIUM

Brussels - Capital Region
5 | The Grand-Place, market square, Brussels
6 | Manneken Pis, Brussels
7 | Belgian Chocolates
8 | Arcades of the Cinquantenaire
9 | The European Parliament
10 | The Royal Galeries St. Hubert
11 | The Marolles, flea market
11 | Street Musicians,
12 | The Eurostar, high speed train Brussels-South
13 | Zinneke Parade, Brussels
13 | Musical Instrument Museum
14 | Brussels Waffles
14 | The Royal Theater Toone (puppets)
15 | The Royal Palace of Brussels
16 | Comic strip trail
16 | The Cathedral of St. Michael and St.Gudula, Brussels
17 | The Atomium, expo 1958

Province of Flemish Brabant/ Province of Walloon Brabant
19 | Landscape between Duisburg and Huldenberg
20 | The Beguinage of Diest
21 | Town Hall of Leuven
22 | Chicory, regional product
23 | Averbode Abbey
24 | National Botanic Garden and the Castle of Bouchout, Meise
25 | Hallerbos (forest), Halle
26 | Jumping, Philippe Lejeune
26 | The Sugarmuseum, Tienen
27 | Geuze, regional bier
28 | Sonian Forest, Tervuren
29 | Brussels Airlines, Belgian national airline
30 | Memorial Day in Waterloo

31 | The Lion's Hillock, Waterloo
32 | The Folon Fondation, La Hulpe
33 | Solvay Park, Castle of La Hulpe
34 | The Hergé Museum, Louvain-la-Neuve
35 | Landscape of Walloon Brabant

Province of Liège
37 | Liège-Guillemins railway station
39 | Museum of Walloon Life
39 | The 'Principautaires', Liège
40 | St. Paul Cathedral, Liège
40 | The 15 August Festival
41 | The Palace of the Prince-Bishops, Liège
42 | 'La Batte', flea market
42 | The Blegny-Mine (coal)
43 | Liège Waffles
44 | Land of Herve
45 | Val Saint-Lambert, Seraing
46 | Reinhardstein Castle
46 | The Thermals of Spa
47 | Spa-Francorchamps, racetrack

Province of Luxembourg
49 | The Giant Tomb, Botassart
50 | The Abbey Orval
51 | The sunset behind the St.- Martin Church of Aarlon
52 | The Basilica of St.-Hubert
53 | The River Semois, Bouillon
54 | Fortified castle of Bouillon
55 | 'Jambon d'Ardenne', smoked ham, St.-Hubert
56 | The smallest town, Durbuy
57 | The lake of Freux
58 | Agricultural festival of Libramont
58 | A game-dish
59 | Book village, Redu

Province of Namur
61 | Landscape with the Abbey of Maredsous
63 | The Citadel of Namur
64 | Festival of Wallonia, waders
65 | Confluence of the Sambre, a river and the Meuse, a stream
66 | Regional Products
67 | Vresse:the creek 'blancs Cailloux'
67 | The brewery of the Abbey St.-Rémy
68 | The Caves of Han
68 | A Rape field
69 | The Citadel and church of Our Lady, Dinant
70 | The Bayard rock, Dinant
70 | Strawberries of Wépion
71 | The Annevoie Gardens
72 | Kayak trip on the Lesse
73 | Carnival in Vierves-sur-Viroin

Province of Hainaut
75 | The Canal du Centre, La Louvière
77 | The Grand-Place, Tournai
78 | Belfry tower of Tournai
78 | Vue from the Strépy-Thieu boatlift
79 | The 'Gilles de Binche'
80 | Musical night of Beloeil
81 | Church Sainte-Waudru, Mons
82 | Center of Mons
83 | Doudou festival, 'Le Lumeçon'
84 | Park Pairi Daiza, Brugelette
84 | The Grand-Hornu
85 | Marsupilami, Charleroi
86 | Seneffe castle
87 | Land of the hills

87	The 'Bois du Cazier', Marcinelle
88	Castle of the Princes, Chimay
89	The lake of l'Eau d'Heure, Boussu-les-Walcourt

Province of West Flanders
91	The North Sea
93	Market Square with provincial Court and Belfry, Bruges
94	Canals of Bruges
95	Procession of the Holy blood, Bruges
96	The port of Zeebrugge
97	Canal of Damme
97	The James Ensor House,Ostend
98	Royal galeries Léopold II, Ostend
99	Mercator port in Ostend
100	'Het Zwin', nature reserve, Knokke
101	Beach cabins, Knokke
102	Flemish grey shrimps
103	Shrimps fishers by horse, Oostduinkerke
104	The Pier of Blankenberge
105	The 'Menenpoort' of Missing Memorial , Ieper
106	The Beguinage of Kortrijk
107	Tram station in De Haan
108	Hops of Poperinge
109	Windsurfing, North Sea

Province of East Flanders
111	Graslei and Korenlei, Ghent
113	The Adoration of the Mystic Lamb, the brothers van Eyck
114	The Azaleas of Ghent area
115	The Belfry, Ghent
116	O'de Flander,gin of the region
117	Flower market, Ghent
118	Castle of the Counts, Ghent

119	Cuberdons, sweet of the region
120	STAM: City Museum Ghent
121	Mola: Provincial Mill Museum, Wachtebeke
122	Ghent: Canal area
123	Mercator statue, Rupelmonde
124	Mattentaarten of Geraards-bergen (regional cake)
125	The Koppenberg(hill), Oudenaarde
126	CRVV:Centre 'Tour of Flanders' Museum, Oudenaarde
127	The polders of St-Laureins
128	Castle of Ooidonk, Deinze
129	Carnival, Aalst

Province of Antwerp
131	City by the Scheldt river, Antwerp
132	The 'Groenplaats' with the Cathedral
133	The Law Courts
134	MAS:Museum on the River, Antwerp
135	The Grote Markt, square market, Antwerp
136	Flandria boat trip, port visit, Antwerp
137	Rubens house, Museum, Antwerp
138	Diamond Museum
139	The Zoo of Antwerp
140	Plantin-Moretus Museum, Antwerp
141	MoMu, Fashion Museum Antwerp
142	'Kalmthoutse Heide', Nature Reserve
143	Klein-Willebroek
144	Skywalk of Mechelen on the St. Rombouts Tower

145	St. Rombouts Cathedral
146	Bobbejaanland, Lichtaart
147	The Postel Abbey cheese
148	Zimmertoren(tower), Lier
149	The Nete, Lier
150	Filet d'Anvers, regional product
151	The Bornem Castle
152	The 'Kabouterberg', Kasterlee
153	Provincial Recreation Park Zilvermeer, Mol

Province of Limburg
155	An orchard in bloom, Haspengouw
157	Apple harvest, Haspengouw
158	Tongeren
158	The National Park Hoge Kempen
159	Open-air Museum Bokrijk
160	Hasselt by night
161	National Gin Museum, Hasselt
162	The marl Caves of Riemst
163	The mining dump, Beringen
164	Blood sausage, a regional speciality
165	The region Maasland
166	Tennis, Kim Clijsters
167	The region Kempenland

169

LÉGENDE MY BELGIUM

La région de Bruxelles-Capitale
5 | La Grand-Place, Bruxelles
6 | Manneken Pis, Bruxelles
7 | Les pralines belges
8 | Arcade du Cinquantenaire
9 | Le Parlement Européen
10 | Galeries Royales Saint-Hubert
11 | Marché aux puces des Marolles
11 | Musiciens de rue
12 | L'Eurostar, train à grande vitesse, Bruxelles-Midi
13 | Zinneke Parade
13 | Musée des Instruments de Musique (MIM)
14 | Gaufres de Bruxelles
14 | Le Théâtre Royal de Toone
15 | Le Palais Royal
16 | Parcours de la Bande dessinée
16 | La cathédrale Saint-Michel et Sainte-Gudule
17 | L'Atomium, expo 1958

Brabant Flamand et Brabant Wallon
19 | Paysage entre Duisburg et Huldenberg
20 | Le Béguinage de Diest
21 | Hôtel de ville de Leuven
22 | Produit du terroir: le chicon
23 | L'Abbaye d'Averbode
24 | Jardin Botanique National et le château de Bouchout, Meise
25 | Hallerbos, Halle
26 | Jumping, Philippe Lejeune
26 | Le Musée du Sucre à Tirlemont
27 | La Gueuze, bière du terroir
28 | Forêt de Soignes, Tervuren
29 | Brussels Airlines, compagnie aérienne nationale

30 | Commémoration: Bataille de Waterloo
31 | Butte du Lion, Waterloo
32 | Fondation Folon, La Hulpe
33 | Domaine Solvay, Château de La Hulpe
34 | Le Musée Hergé à Louvain-la-Neuve
35 | Paysage hivernal du Brabant Wallon

Province de Liège
37 | Gare Liège-Guillemins
39 | Musée de la Vie Wallonne
39 | Les Principautaires, Liège
40 | Cathédrale Saint-Paul
40 | La fête du 15 août à Liège
41 | Palais des Princes-Evêques
42 | Marché de La Batte, Liège
42 | La mine de Blegny
43 | Gaufres de Liège
44 | Pays de Herve
45 | Val Saint-Lambert, Seraing
46 | Château Reinhardstein
46 | Les Thermes de Spa
47 | Spa-Francorchamps, circuit automobile

Province du Luxembourg
49 | Tombeau du Géant, Botassart
50 | L'Abbaye d'Orval
51 | Coucher de soleil derrière Saint-Martin, Aarlon
52 | La Basilique Saint-Hubert à St.-Hubert
53 | La Semois à Bouillon
54 | Château-Fort de Bouillon
55 | Jambon d'Ardenne, St.-Hubert
56 | La plus petite ville: Durbuy
57 | Les étangs de Freux

58 | Foire agricole de Libramont
58 | Un plat de gibier
59 | Redu: village du livre

Province de Namur
61 | Paysage avec l'Abbaye de Maredsous
63 | Citadelle de Namur
64 | Fête de la Wallonie, les échasseurs
65 | Confluent de la Meuse et la Sambre
66 | Produits du terroir
67 | Ruisseau des Blancs Cailloux, Vresse
67 | Brasserie de l'Abbaye St.-Rémy
68 | Grottes de Han
68 | Un champ de Colza
69 | Citadelle et Collégiale Notre-Dame de Dinant
70 | Rocher Bayard, Dinant
70 | Les fraises de Wépion
71 | Jardins d'Annevoie
72 | Descente de la Lesse, kayak
73 | Carnaval à Vierves-sur-Viroin

Province du Hainaut
75 | Canal du Centre , La Louvière
77 | Grand-Place, Tournai
78 | Beffroi, Tournai
78 | Strépy-Thieu: ascenseur funiculaire
79 | Les Gilles de Binche
80 | Nuit musicale à Beloeil
81 | Collégiale Sainte-Waudru, Mons
82 | Centre ville de Mons
83 | Fête Doudou, le Lumeçon
84 | Brugelette: parc Pairi Daiza
84 | Le Grand-Hornu
85 | Marsupilami à Charleroi
86 | Château de Seneffe
87 | Pays des Collines

87 | Le Bois du cazier à marcinelle
88 | Château des Princes , Chimay
89 | Les lacs de l'Eau d'Heure,
     Boussu-lez-Walcourt

**Province de la
Flandre Occidentale**
91 | La Mer du Nord
93 | La Grand-Place: Palais
     Provincial et le Beffroi, Bruges
94 | Les canaux de Bruges
95 | Procession du Saint-Sang
96 | Port de Zeebrugge
97 | Canal de Damme
97 | Maison de James Ensor (musée),
     à Ostende
98 | Galeries Royales Léopold II,
     Ostende
99 | Le port Mercator, Ostende
100 | Réserve naturelle; le Zwin
101 | Cabines de plage à Knokke
102 | Crevettes grises flamandes
103 | La pêche aux crevettes,
     Oostduinkerke
104 | Le' Pier' de Blankenberge
105 | Porte de Menin, Ypres
106 | Béguinage de Courtrai
107 | Arrêt de tram, De Haan
108 | Le Houblon, Poperinge
109 | Windsurfing, Mer du nord

**Province de la Flandre
Orientale**
111 | Quai aux Herbes et Quai aux
     Grains, Gand
113 | L'Adoration de l'Agneau
     Mystique, les frères Van Eyck,
     Gand
114 | Azalées de la région gantoise
115 | Le beffroi de Gand
116 | O'de Flander, genièvre

117 | Marché aux fleurs, Gand
118 | Château des Comtes, Gand
119 | Cuberdons, produit du terroir
120 | STAM: musée de la
     ville de Gand
121 | Mola: musée provincial du Moulin
     à Wachtebeke
122 | Zone industrielle du
     Canal de Gand
123 | Mercator, Rupelmonde
124 | Mattentaarten de
     Geraardsbergen
125 | Koppenberg, Oudenaarde
126 | CRVV: Centre du Tour de
     Flandre, Oudenaarde
127 | Polders de Sint-Laureins
128 | Château de Ooidonk, Deinze
129 | Le carnaval d'Alost

Province d'Anvers
131 | Anvers à la rive de l'Escaut
132 | Groenplaats avec la
     cathédrale Notre-Dame
133 | Tribunal de justice, Anvers
134 | MAS:Musée le long du fleuve
135 | La Grand-Place, Anvers
136 | Flandria, le port d'Anvers
137 | La Maison de Rubens, Anvers
138 | Musée du Diamant, Anvers
139 | Zoo d'Anvers
140 | Musée Plantin-Moretus,
     Anvers
141 | MoMu: Musée de la Mode
142 | Réserve naturelle:
     Kalmthoutse Heide
143 | Klein-Willebroek
144 | Skywalk: la tour St.-Rombout,
     Malines
145 | Cathédrale St.-Rombout
146 | Bobbejaanland, Lichtaart
147 | Fromage de l'Abbaye de Postel

148 | Zimmertoren (tour), Lier
149 | La Nèthe, Lier
150 | Filet d'Anvers
151 | Château de Bornem
152 | Kabouterberg, Kasterlee
153 | Domaine récréatif provincial:
     het Zilvermeer, Mol

Province du Limbourg
155 | Verger en fleurs: Haspengouw
157 | Récolte de pommes,
     Haspengouw
158 | Tongres
158 | Le Parc National de
     la Haute Campine
159 | Musée en plein air de Bokrijk
160 | Hasselt by night
161 | Musée National du Genièvre,
     Hasselt
162 | Grottes de Kanne, Riemst
163 | Mijnterril (mine), Beringen
164 | Boudin noir des Fourons
165 | Maasland (la Meuse)
166 | Tennis: Kim Clijsters
167 | La Haute Campine

LEGENDE MY BELGIUM

Brussels Hoofdstedelijk Gewest

5 Grote Markt, Brussel
6 Manneken Pis, Brussel
7 Belgische pralines
8 Arcades van het Jubelpark
9 Europees Parlement
10 Koninklijke Sint-Hubertus galerijen
11 Vlooienmarkt van de Marollen
11 Straatmuzikanten
12 De Eurostar, hoge snelheidstrein, Brussel-Zuid
13 Zinneke Parade
13 Het Muziekinstrumentenmuseum
14 Brusselse wafels
14 Koninklijk Poppentheater Toone
15 Koninklijk Paleis
16 Stripwandeling
16 St.-Michielsen en St.-Goedele-kathedraal
17 Het Atomium, expo 1958

Vlaams-Brabant en Waals-Brabant

19 Landschap tussen Duisburg en Huldenberg
20 Begijnhof van Diest
21 Het Stadhuis van Leuven
22 Streekproduct: witloof
23 De Abdij van Averbode
24 Nationale Plantentuin en het Kasteel van Bouchout in Meise
25 Het Hallerbos, Halle
26 Jumping, Philippe Lejeune
26 Het Suikermuseum van Tienen
27 Geuze, een streekbier
28 Het Zoniënwoud , Tervuren
29 Brussels Airlines, nationale luchtvaartmaatschappij,

30 Herdenking: Slag bij Waterloo
31 Leeuwenheuvel, Waterloo
32 Stichting Folon, Terhulpen
33 Domein Solvay, Kasteel van La Hulpe
34 Het Hergé-museum in Louvain-la-Neuve
35 Winterlandschap Waals-Brabant

Provincie Luik

37 Het station van Luik-Guillemins
39 Museum van het Waalse Leven
39 Les Principautaires' , Luik
40 Sint-Pauluskathedraal
40 Het feest van de 15de augustus
41 Prinsbisschoppelijk Paleis,Luik
42 De markt 'La Batte' in Luik
42 De mijn van Blegny
43 Luikse Wafels
44 Land van Herve
45 Val Saint-Lambert, Seraing
46 Kasteel Reinhardstein
46 Thermen van Spa
47 Spa-Francorchamps, autorace

Provincie Luxemburg

49 Graf van de Reus in Botassart
50 Abdij van Orval
51 Zonsondergang achter de Sint-Maartenskerk van Aarlen
52 Sint-Hubertusbasiliek in St. Hubert
53 De Semois bij Bouillon
54 Versterkt kasteel van Bouillon
55 Ardeense hesp in St. Hubert
56 Kleinste stad: Durbuy
57 De vijvers van Freux
58 Landbouwbeurs van Libramont
58 Een wildgerecht
59 Redu: boekendorp

Provincie Namen

61 Landschap met de abdij van Maredsous
63 Citadel van Namen
64 Waalse feesten, steltlopers
65 Samenvloeiing van de Maas en de Samber
66 Lokale streekprodukten
67 Blancs Cailloux,Vresse
67 De brouwerij van de abdij St.-Rémy
68 De Grotten van Han
68 Een koolzaadveld
69 Citadel en collegiale kerk Onze-Lieve-Vrouw, Dinant
70 Rots Bayard, Dinant
70 Aardbeien van Wépion
71 Tuinen van Annevoie
72 Afvaart van de Lesse , kajak
73 Carnaval in Vierves-sur-Viroin

Provincie Henegouwen

75 Het Centrumkanaal, ter hoogte van La Louvière
77 Grote Markt, Doornik
78 Belfort van Doornik
78 Strépy-Thieu; scheepslift
79 Gilles van Binche
80 Muzikale nacht in Beloeil
81 Collegiale Sint-Waltrudiskerk, Bergen
82 Stadscentrum van Bergen
83 'Doudou-feest', le Lumeçon
84 Brugelette, park Pairi Daiza
84 Grand-Hornu
85 Marsupilami in Charleroi
86 Kasteel van Seneffe
87 Heuvelland
87 Bois du Cazier' in Marcinelle
88 Prinsenkasteel in Chimay
89 De meren van L'Eau d'Heure: Boussu-lez-Walcourt

West-Vlaanderen
91 De Noordzee
93 Grote Markt met Provinciaal
   Hof en het Belfort, Brugge
94 Kanalen van Brugge
95 Heilige Bloedprocessie,Brugge
96 Haven van Zeebrugge
97 Kanaal van Damme
97 James Ensorhuis (museum)
   in Oostende
98 Koninklijke gaanderijen
   Leopold II, Oostende
99 Mercator Haven
100 Natuurreservaat: Het Zwin
101 Strandcabines in Knokke
102 Vlaamse grijze garnalen
103 Garnalenvangst Oostduinkerke
104 Pier van Blankenberge
105 Menenpoort, Ieper
106 Begijnhof van Kortrijk
107 Tramstation in De Haan
108 Poperingse hop
109 Windsurfing op de Noordzee

Provincie Oost-Vlaanderen
111 Gras- en Korenlei, Gent
113 Het Lam Gods,
   gebroeders Van Eyck, Gent
114 Gentse Azalea
115 Het Belfort van Gent
116 O'de Flander, graanjenever
117 Bloemenmarkt, Gent
118 Het Gravensteen, Gent
119 Cuberdons, streekprodukt
120 STAM:Stadsmuseum-Gent
121 Mola: Provinciaal
   Molencentrum in Wachtebeke
122 Gentse kanaalzone
123 Mercator , Rupelmonde
124 Geraardsbergse mattentaarten
125 Koppenberg, Oudenaarde

126 CRVV: Centrum Ronde
   Van Vlaanderen, Oudenaarde
127 Polders van Sint-Laureins
128 Kasteel van Ooidonk, Deinze
129 Carnaval van Aalst

Provincie Antwerpen
131 Antwerpen aan de Schelde
132 Groenplaats met
   Onze-Lieve-Vrouwkathedraal
133 Gerechtsgebouw
134 MAS:Museum aan de stroom
135 De Grote Markt, Antwerpen
136 Flandria; rondvaart in de
   haven van Antwerpen
137 Het Rubenshuis, Antwerpen
138 Diamantenmuseum,Antwerpen
139 Zoo van Antwerpen
140 Plantin-Moretusmuseum
141 MoMu: Mode Museum
142 Kalmthoutse Heide,
   natuurreservaat
143 Klein-Willebroek
144 Skywalk van Mechelen,
   vanop de Sint-Romboutstoren
145 Sint-Romboutskathedraal
146 Bobbejaanland, Lichtaart
147 Abdijkaas van Postel
148 Zimmertoren, Lier
149 Binnennete, Lier
150 Filet d'Anvers
151 Kasteel van Bornem
152 Kabouterberg, Kasterlee
153 Provinciaal Recreatiedomein:
   het Zilvermeer , Mol

Provincie Limburg
155 Bloesems in Haspengouw
157 Appeloogst, Haspengouw
158 Tongeren
158 Nationaal Park de Hoge Kempen

159 Openluchtmuseum Bokrijk
160 Hasselt by night
161 Nationaal Jenevermuseum,
   Hasselt
162 Mergelgrotten, Riemst
163 Mijnterril, Beringen
164 Voerense trip, bloedworst
165 Maasland
166 Tennis: Kim Clijsters
167 Kempenland

LEGENDEN MY BELGIUM

Brüssel-Hauptstadtregion
5 Grand-Place, Brüssel
6 Manneken Pis, Brüssel
7 Die belgischen Pralinen
8 Arkaden des Cinquantenaire
9 Das Europaparlament
10 Königliche Galerien
   St. Hubertus
11 Flohmarkt der Marollen
11 Straßenmusikanten
12 Der Eurostar, Hochgeschwin-
   digkeitszug, Brüssel-Süd
13 Zinneke Parade
13 Musikinstrumenten-
   museum (MIM)
14 Brüsseler Waffeln
14 Das königliche Marionetten-
   theater Toone
15 Der Königspalast
16 Der Comic-Rundweg
16 Die Kathedrale St. Michael
   und St. Gudula
17 Atomium , Expo 1958

**Flämisch Brabant /
Wallonisch Brabant**
19 Landschaft zwischen Duisburg
   und Huldenberg
20 Beginenhof in Diest
21 Rathaus Leuven
22 Das Landesprodukt: Chicorée
23 Die Abtei in Averbode
24 Nationaler Botanischer Garten
   und Schloss Bouchout, Meise
25 Wald bei Halle
26 Springreiter Philippe Lejeune
26 Das Zuckermuseum, Tienen
27 Geuze, Bier aus der Region
28 Zoniënwoud (Wald), Tervuren
29 Brussels Airlines, nationale
   Fluggesellschaft

30 Gedenktag für die Schlacht bei
   Waterloo
31 Der 'Löwe von Waterloo'
32 Die Stiftung Folon, La Hulpe
33 Domäne Solvay, Schloss von
   La Hulpe
34 Das Hergé-Museum in
   Louvain-la Neuve
35 Winterlandschaft
   Wallonisch Brabant

Provinz Lüttich
37 Der Bahnhof Lüttich-Guillemins
39 Wallonisches Museum
   für Volkskunde
39 'Les Principautaires', Lüttich
40 Kathedrale St. Paul
40 Fest des 15. August,
   Lüttich
41 Palast der Fürstbischöfe
42 Der Markt La Batte, Lüttich
42 Bergwerk in Blegny
43 Lütticher Waffeln
44 Herver Land
45 Val Saint-Lambert, Seraing
46 Die Burg Reinhardstein
46 Die Thermen von Spa
47 Spa-Francorchamps,
   Autorennen

Provinz Luxemburg
49 Riesengrab, Botassart
50 Die Abtei von Orval
51 Sonnenuntergang hinter
   der St. Martinskirche, Aarlon
52 St. Hubertus Basilika
53 Der Fluss Semois bei Bouillon
54 Festung von Bouillon
55 Ardenner Schinken, St. Hubert
56 Die kleinste Stadt: Durbuy
57 Der See von Freux

58 Landwirtschaftmesse in
   Libramont
58 Ein Wildgericht
59 Redu: Bücherdorf

Provinz Namur
61 Landschaft mit der
   Abtei von Maredsous
63 Zitadelle von Namur
64 Festival von Wallonien,
   die Stelzenläufer
65 Zusammenfluss
   von Maas und Sambre
66 Regionale Produkte
67 Der Bach Blancs Cailloux
   bei Vresse
67 Brauerei der Abtei Saint-Rémy
68 Die Grotten von Han
68 Ein Rapsfeld
69 Zitadelle und Stiftskirche
   Notre-Dame, Dinant
70 Die Bayard-Felsen, Dinant
70 Erdbeeren von Wépion
71 Die Gärten von Annevoie
72 Kajakfahrt auf der Lesse
73 Karneval, Vierves-sur-Viroin

Provinz Hainaut
75 Der Canal du Centre,
   La Louvière
77 Grand-Place, Tournai
78 Der Belfried, Tournai
78 Schiffshebewerk Strépy-Thieu
79 Die 'Gilles de Binche'
80 Musikalische Nacht, Beloeil
81 Stiftskirche Sainte-Waudru, Mons
82 Das Stadtzentrum von Mons
83 Doudou-Fest, 'Le Lumeçon'
84 Brugelette: Park Pairi Daiza
84 Grand-Hornu
85 Marsupilami in Charleroi

174

86	Das Schloss von Seneffe
87	Die Region Hügelland
87	'Bois du Cazier', Marcinelle
88	Prinzenschloss in Chimay
89	Die Seen von l'Eau d'Heure, Boussu-lez-Walcourt

Provinz West-Flandern
91	Die Nordsee
93	Markt mit dem Provinzialhof und dem Belfried, Brügge
94	Die Kanäle von Brügge
95	Heiligblutprozession, Brügge
96	Hafen Zeebrügges
97	Kanal von Damme
97	Das James Ensor Haus (Museum), Ostende
98	Königliche Galerie Leopold II, Ostende
99	Mercatorhafen, Ostende
100	Naturreservat: Het Zwin
101	Strandkabinen in Knokke
102	Graue flämische Garnelen
103	Die Garnelenfischer zu Pferd, Oostduinkerke
104	Der 'Pier' von Blankenberge
105	Menen-Tor, Ypern
106	Beginenhof, Kortrijk
107	Tramhaltestelle in De Haan
108	Hopfen bei Poperinge
109	Windsurfen an der Nordsee

Provinz Ost-Flandern
111	Graslei und Korenlei, Gent
113	Anbetung des Lamm Gottes, die Brüder Van Eyck, Gent
114	Azaleen in der Region Gent
115	Der Belfried von Gent
116	O'de Flander, Genever
117	Blumenmarkt in Gent
118	Der Gravensteen, Gent

119	Cuberdons, Süßigkeit
120	STAM: Museum der Stadt Gent
121	Mola: Mühlenmuseum in Wachtebeke
122	Kanalzone Gent
123	Mercator, Rupelmonde
124	Mattentaarten von Geraardsbergen (Kuchen)
125	Koppenberg, Oudenaarde
126	CRVV: Zentrum 'Flandernrund-fahrt', Oudenaarde
127	Die Polder von St. Laureins
128	Schloss Ooidonk, Deinze
129	Karneval in Aalst

Provinz Antwerpen
131	Antwerpen am Scheldeufer
132	Groenplaats mit der Liebfrauenkathedrale
133	Justizgebäude, Antwerpen
134	MAS: Museum am Strom
135	Der Grote Markt, Antwerpen
136	Flandria: Hafenrundfahrt, Antwerpen
137	Rubenshaus, Museum
138	Das Diamantenmuseum
139	Der Zoo von Antwerpen
140	Plantin-Moretus-Museum
141	MoMu: Das Modemuseum, Antwerpen
142	Kalmthoutser Heide, ein Naturschutzgebiet
143	Klein-Willebroek
144	Skywalk auf dem St. Romboutsturm, Mechelen
145	St.Romboutskathedrale
146	Bobbejaanland, Lichtaart
147	Abteikäse aus Postel
148	Zimmerturm, Lier

149	Die Nete, Lier
150	Filet d'Anvers, eine Spezialität
151	Schloss von Bornem
152	Kabouterberg, Kasterlee
153	Erholungspark der Provinz: Zilvermeer, Mol

Provinz Limburg
155	Blütenpracht in Haspengau
157	Apfelernte in Haspengau
158	Tongern
158	Nationalpark Hoge Kempen
159	Freilichtmuseum, Bokrijk
160	Hasselt by night
161	Nationales Genevermuseum, Hasselt
162	Mergelgrotten, Riemst
163	Bergbauhalden, Beringen
164	Blutwurst, Voeren-Region
165	Maasland
166	Tennis: Kim Clijsters
167	Kempenland

LEYENDAS MY BELGIUM

Región de Bruselas-Capital
5 La Grand Place, Bruselas
6 Manneken Pis, Bruselas
7 Bombones belgas
8 Arcadas del Cincuentenario
9 Parlamento Europeo
10 Galerías Reales
   de San Hubert
11 Mercadillo de los Marolles
11 Músicos en la calle,
12 El tren de alta velocidad
   Eurostar, Bruselas Sur
13 Desfile de Zinneke, Bruselas
13 Museo de instrumentos musicales
14 Gofres de Bruselas
14 Teatro Real de Toone
   (marionetas)
15 Palacio Real
16 Ruta de los cómics
16 Catedral de San Miguel
   y Santa Gúdula, Bruselas
17 El Atomium, expo de 1958

**Provincia del Brabante
Flamenco/ Provincia
del Brabante Valón**
19 Paisaje entre Duisburgo
   y Huldenberg
20 Beguinaje de Diest
21 Ayuntamiento de Lovaina
22 Endibia, producto regional
23 Abadía de Averbode
24 Jardín Botánico Nacional
   Castillo de Bouchout, Meise
25 bosque, Halle
26 Jinete de saltos, Philippe Lejeune
26 Museo del azúcar, Tienen
27 Geuze, cerveza regional
28 Bosque de Soignes, Tervuren
29 Brussels Airlines,
   compañía aérea nacional belga

30 Día de conmemoración de la
   batalla de Waterloo
31 El león de Waterloo
32 Fundación Folon, La Hulpe
33 Parque Solvay,
   Castillo de La Hulpe
34 Museo Hergé, Lovaina la Nueva
35 Paisaje de invierno
   del Brabante Valón

Provincia de Lieja
37 Estación de tren de
   Lieja-Guillemins
39 Museo de la vida valona
39 Les «Principautaires», Lieja
40 Catedral de San Pablo, Lieja
40 Festividad del 15 de agosto
41 Palacio de los
   Príncipes-Obispos
42 Mercadillo de «La Batte», Lieja
42 Mina de Blegny
43 Gofres de Lieja
44 Región de Herve
45 Valle de Saint-Lambert,
   Seraing
46 Castillo de Reinhardstein
46 Termas de Spa
47 Spa-Francorchamps, circuito

Provincia de Luxemburgo
49 Tumba del Gigante, Botassart
50 Abadía de Orval
51 Puesta de sol tras la
   Iglesia de San Martín de Aarlon
52 Basílica de San Hubert
53 Río Semois, Bouillon
54 Castillo fortificado de Bouillon
55 «Jambon d'Ardenne»,
   jamón ahumado, San Hubert
56 La ciudad más pequeña,
   Durbuy

57 Lago de Freux
58 Feria de agricultura de Libramont y un plato de caza
59 Ciudad de los libros, Redu

Provincia de Namur
61 Paisaje con la Abadía
   de Maredsous
63 Ciudadela de Namur
64 Festival de Valonia,
   "les échasseurs"
65 Confluencia del Sambre,
   y el Mosa
66 Productos regionales
67 Vresse: arroyo «blancs Cailloux»
67 Fábrica de cerveza de la Abadía
   de St.Rémy
68 Grutas de Han
68 Campo de colza
69 Ciudadela e Iglesia de
   Nuestra Señora, Dinant
70 Roca de Bayard, Dinant
70 Fresas de Wépion
71 Jardines de Annevoie
72 Excursión en kayak por el Lesse
73 Carnaval de Vierves-sur-Viroin

Provincia de Henao
75 Canal del Centro, La Louvière
77 La Grand Place, Tournai
78 Campanario de Tournai
78 Vista desde el funicular de
   Strépy-Thieu
79 Los «Gilles de Binche»
80 Noche musical de Beloeil
81 Iglesia de Sainte-Waudru, Mons
82 Centro de Mons
83 Festival de Doudou,
   «Le Lumeçon»
84 Parque Pairi Daiza, Brugelette
84 El Grand-Hornu

85 | Marsupilami, Charleroi
86 | Castillo de Seneffe
87 | Región de las colinas
87 | «Bois du Cazier», Marcinelle
88 | Castillo de los Príncipes, Chimay
89 | Lago de l'Eau d'Heure, Boussu-les-Walcourt

Flandes Occidental
91 | Mar del Norte
93 | Plaza del mercado con Audiencia provincial y campanario, Brujas
94 | Canales de Brujas
95 | Procesión de la Santa Sangre, Brujas
96 | Puerto de Zeebrugge
97 | Canal de Damme
97 | Casa James Ensor (museo), Ostende
98 | Galerías Reales de Leopoldo II, Ostende
99 | Puerto Mercator en Ostende
100 | «Het Zwin», reserva natural
101 | Casetas de playa, Knokke
102 | Gambas grises flamencas
103 | Pescadores de gambas a caballo, Oostduinkerke
104 | Muelle de Blankenberge
105 | La «Menenpoort» en memoria de los caídos, Ypres
106 | Beguinaje de Kortrijk
107 | Estación de tranvía de De Haan
108 | Lúpulo de Poperinge
109 | Windsurfing, Mar del Norte

Provincia de Flandes Oriental
111 | Calles Graslei y Korenlei, Gante
113 | La Adoración del Cordero Místico, de los hermanos van Ey
114 | Azaleas de la zona de Gante
115 | Campanario de Gante
116 | O'de Flander, ginebra
117 | Mercado de las flores, Gante
118 | Castillo de los Condes, Gante
119 | Cuberdons, dulces de la región
120 | STAM: Museo de la ciudad de Gante
121 | Mola: Museo del molino, Wachtebeke
122 | Gante: zona del canal
123 | Mercator, Rupelmonde
124 | Mattentaarten de Geraardsbergen (tarta regional)
125 | El Koppenberg, Oudenaarde
126 | CRVV: Centro del Tour de Flandes, Oudenaarde
127 | Polders de St. Laureins
128 | Castillo de Ooidonk, Deinze
129 | Carnaval, Aalst

Provincia de Amberes
131 | Ciudad a orillas del río Escalda, Amberes
132 | El «Groenplaats» con la Catedral
133 | Tribunal de Justicia
134 | MAS: Museo del río
135 | El Grote Markt, Amberes
136 | Excursión en barco Flandria, visita al puerto, Amberes
137 | Casa de Rubens, Amberes
138 | Museo del diamante
139 | Zoo de Amberes
140 | Museo Plantin-Moretus
141 | MoMu, Museo de la moda, Amberes
142 | «Kalmthoutse Heide», reserva natural
143 | Klein-Willebroek
144 | Skywalk de la torre de San Rumoldo en Malinas
145 | Catedral de San Rumoldo
146 | Bobbejaanland, Lichtaart
147 | Queso de la Abadía de Postel
148 | Torre Zimmer, Lier
149 | El Nete, Lier
150 | Filet d'Anvers, producto regional
151 | Castillo de Bornem
152 | El «Kabouterberg», Kasterlee
153 | Parque recreativo provincial Zilvermeer, Mol

Provincia de Limburgo
155 | Huerto en flor, Haspengouw
157 | Cosecha de la manzana, Haspengouw
158 | Tongeren
158 | Parque nacional Hoge Kempen
159 | Museo al aire libre de Bokrijk
160 | Hasselt de noche
161 | Museo Nacional de la Ginebra, Hasselt
162 | Cuevas de marga de Riemst
163 | Mina abandonada, Beringen
164 | Morcilla, especialidad regional de Voeren
165 | La región de Maasland
166 | Tenis, Kim Clijsters
167 | Kempenland

DIDASCALIE MY BELGIUM

Bruxelles – Regione della Capitale
5 La Grand-Place,
   Piazza del mercato, Bruxelles
6 Manneken Pis, Bruxelles
7 Cioccolato belga
8 Arcate del Cinquantenario
9 Parlamento Europeo
10 Gallerie Reali St. Hubert
11 Il Marolles, mercatino
   delle pulci
11 Musicanti di strada,
12 L'Eurostar, treno ad alta velocità
   Bruxelles-Sud
13 Sfilata Zinneke, Bruxelles
13 Museo degli strumenti musicali
14 I wafer di Bruxelles
14 Teatro Reale Toone (burattini)
15 Palazzo Reale di Bruxelles
16 Il percorso dei fumetti
16 Cattedrale di S. Michele
   e di St. Gudula, Bruxelles
17 L'Atomium, expo 1958

Provincia del Brabante Fiammingo/Provincia del Brabante Vallone
19 Paesaggio tra Duisburg
   e Huldenberg
20 Il Beguinage di Diest
21 Municipio di Lovanio
22 Cicoria, prodotto regionale
23 Abbazia di Averbode
24 Giardino Botanico Nazionale
   Castello di Bouchout, Meise
25 Hallerbos (foresta), Halle
26 Jumping, Philippe Lejeune
26 The Sugarmuseum (il Museo
   dello Zucchero), Tienen
27 La Geuze, birra regionale
28 Sonian Forest, Tervuren

29 Brussels Airlines, compagnia
   aerea di bandiera belga
30 Memorial Day a Waterloo
31 The Lion's Hillock, Waterloo
32 La Folon Fondation, La Hulpe
33 Solvay Park, Castello di La Hulpe
34 Hergé Museum,
   Louvain-la-Neuve
35 Paesaggio del Brabante Vallone

Provincia di Liegi
37 Liegi-Guillemins
   Stazione ferroviaria
39 Museo della vita vallona
39 Il "Principautaires", Liegi
40 Cattedrale di S. Paolo, Liegi
40 Il Festival del 15 agosto
41 Palazzo del
   Principe-Arcivescovo, Liegi
42 "La Batte", mercatino delle pulci
42 Miniera di Blegny (carbone)
43 Wafer di Liegi
44 La Terra di Herve
45 Val Saint-Lambert, Seraing
46 Castello di Reinhardstein
46 Le Terme della Spa
47 Circuito di Spa-Francorchamps

Provincia di Lussemburgo
49 La Tomba del Gigante,
   Botassart
50 Abbazia di Orval
51 Tramonto dietro la
   Chiesa di S. Martino di Aarlon
52 Basilica di S. Uberto
53 Il fiume Semois, Bouillon
54 Fortezza di Bouillon
55 "Jambon d'Ardenne",
   prosciutto affumicato. St.-Hubert
56 La città più piccola, Durbuy
57 Il lago di Freux

58 Festival dell'agricoltura
   di Libramont
59 Book village, Redu

Provincia di Namur
61 Paesaggio con l'abbazia
   di Maredsous
63 La Cittadella di Namur
64 Festival della Vallonia,
   "les échasseurs"
65 Confluenza della Sambre, un
   fiume, e la Meuse, un ruscello
66 Prodotti regionali
67 Vresse: il torrente "blancs
   Cailloux"
67 La birreria dell'abbazia
   di St.-Rémy
68 Le Grotte di Han
68 Un campo di rape
69 Cittadella e chiesa
   della Nostra Signora, Dinant
70 La roccia di Bayard, Dinant
70 Fragole di Wépion
71 I giardini di Annevoie
72 Escursione in kayak
   sul fiume Lesse
73 Carnevale a Vierves-sur-Viroin

Provincia dell'Hainaut
75 Canal du Centre, La Louvière
77 Grand-Place, Tournai
78 La Torre Belfry di Tournai
78 Veduta dal boatlift di Strépy-Thieu
79 "Gilles de Binche"
80 Notte musicale di Beloeil
81 Chiesa di Sainte-Waudru, Mons
82 Centro di Mons
83 Doudou Festival, "Le Lumeçon"
84 Parco Pairi Daiza, Brugelette
84 Il Grand-Hornu
85 Marsupilami, Charleroi

86	Castello di Seneffe
87	La terra delle colline
87	Il "Bois du Cazier", Marcinelle
88	Castello della Principessa, Chimay
89	Il lago di l'Eau d'Heure, Boussu-les-Walcourt

Fiandre Occidentali

91	Il Mare del Nord
93	Piazza del mercato con la Corte provinciale e Belfry, Bruges
94	Canali di Bruges
95	Processione del Sangue santo, Bruges
96	Il porto di Zeebrugge
97	Il Canale di Damme
97	La Casa di James Ensor, Ostenda
98	Gallerie reali Léopold II, Ostenda
99	Il porto mercantile di Ostenda
100	"Het Zwin", riserva naturale, Knokke
101	Cabine sulla spiaggia, Knokke
102	Gamberetti grigi fiamminghi
103	Pescatori di gamberetti a cavallo, Oostduinkerke
104	Molo di Blankenberge
105	Il "Menenpoort" del Missing Memorial, Ieper
106	Il Beguinage di Kortrijk
107	Stazione del tram a De Haan
108	Luppolo di Poperinge
109	Windsurf nel Mare del Nord

Provincia delle Fiandre Orientali

111	Graslei e Korenlei, Gand
113	L'adorazione dell'Agnello mistico, i fratelli van Eyck
114	Azalee della zona intorno a Gand

115	Il Belfry, Gand
116	O'de Flander, il gin della regione
117	Mercato dei fiori di Gand
118	Castello delle Conti, Gand
119	Il Cuberdons, dolce tipico regionale
120	STAM: il Museo della Città di Gand
121	Mola: Museo Provinciale dei mulini a vento, Wachtebeke
122	Gand: la zona del canale
123	Statua di Mercator, Rupelmonde
124	Mattentaarten di Geraardsbergen (torta regionale)
125	La collina Koppenberg, Oudenaarde
126	CRVV: Centro Museo "Tour delle Fiandre", Oudenaarde
127	I polder di St-Laureins
128	Castello di Ooidonk, Deinze
129	Il Carnevale di Aalst

Provincia di Anversa

131	Veduta della città dalla Schelda, Anversa
132	I "Groenplaats" con la Cattedrale
133	Il Palazzo di Giustizia
134	MAS: il Museo sul fiume, Anversa
135	Il Mercato di Grote, mercato in piazza, Anversa
136	Gita in barca per le Fiandre, visita al porto, Anversa
137	Rubens house, Museo, Anversa
138	Il Museo dei Diamanti
139	Lo Zoo di Anversa
140	Plantin-Moretus Museum, Anversa
141	MoMu, il Museo della moda, Anversa

142	"Kalmthoutse Heide", riserva naturale
143	Klein-Willebroek
144	Skywalk di Mechelen sulla Torre di St. Rombouts
145	Cattedrale di St. Rombouts
146	Bobbejaanland, Lichtaart
147	Formaggio dell'Abbazia di Postel
148	Zimmertoren (torre), Lier
149	Il Nete, Lier
150	Filet d'Anvers, prodotto regionale
151	Il Castello di Bornem
152	Il "Kabouterberg", Kasterlee
153	Parco ricreativo provinciale Zilvermeer, Mol

Provincia di Limburgo

155	Un'orchidea in fiore sbocciando, Haspengouw
157	La raccolta delle mele, Haspengouw
158	Tongeren
158	Parco Nazionale di Hoge Kempen
159	Museo open-air di Bokrijk
160	Hasselt di notte
161	Museo Nazionale di Gin, Hasselt
162	Grotte di marna a Riemst
163	La discarica della miniera, Beringen
164	Tipo di sanguinaccio, una specialità regionale
165	La regione di Maasland
166	Tennis, Kim Clijsters
167	La regione di Kempenland

LEGENDAS MY BELGIUM

A região de Bruxelas - Capital
5 A Praça Grande, praça do
  Mercado, Bruxelas
6 Manneken Pis, Bruxelas
7 Os chocolates belgas
8 Arcadas do Cinquentenário
9 O Parlamento Europeu
10 As Galerias Reais St. Hubert
11 Feira da Ladra Marolles
11 Músicos de rua, Museu dos
12 O Eurostar, comboio de alta
   velocidade, Bruxelas Sul
13 Zinneke Parade, Bruxelas
13 Instrumentos Musicais
14 Bolachas de Bruxelas
14 O Teatro Real de Toone
   (marionetas)
15 O Palácio Real de Bruxelas
16 Percurso da Banda Desenhada
16 A Catedral de Saint Michel
   e Santa Gudula
17 O Atomium, expo 1958

**Província do Brabante
Flamengo/ Província do
Brabante Valão**
19 Paisagem entre Duisburg
   e Huldenberg
20 A Beguinaria de Diest
21 Câmara Municipal de Leuven
22 A endívia, produto regional
23 Abadia de Averbode
24 Jardim Botânico Nacional
   Castelo de Bouchout, Meise
25 Hallerbos (floresta), Halle
26 Jumping, Philippe Lejeune
26 O Museu do Açúcar, Tienen
27 Geuze, cerveja regional
28 Floresta Sonian, Tervuren
29 Brussels Airlines,
   Companhia Aérea Nacional

30 Comemoração em Waterloo
31 A Colina do Leão, Waterloo
32 A Fundação Folon, La Hulpe
33 Parque Solvay,
   Castelo de La Hulpe
34 Museu Hergé,
   Louvain-la-Neuve
35 Paisagem do Brabante Valão

Província de Liège
37 Liège-Guillemins
   Estação de Caminhos-de-ferro
39 Museu da Vida da Valónia
39 Os ,Principautaires', Liège
40 A Catedral de São Paulo,
   Liège
40 O Festival de 15 de Agosto
41 O Palácio dos
   Príncipes-Bispos, Liège
42 'La Batte', feira da ladra
42 A mina Blegny (carvão)
43 Bolachas de Liège
44 País de Herve
45 Vale Saint-Lambert, Seraing
46 Castelo Reinhardstein
46 As Termas de Spa
47 Spa-Francorchamps,
   circuito automóvel

Província de Luxemburgo
49 O Túmulo do Gigante,
   Botassart
50 A Abadia de Orval
51 Pôr-do-sol por trás da Igreja de
   Saint Martin de Aarlon
52 A Basílica de St.-Hubert
53 O Rio Semois, Bouillon
54 Castelo Fortificado
   de Bouillon
55 'Presunto das Ardenas',
   Presunto fumado, St.-Hubert

56 A cidade mais pequena,
   Durbuy
57 O Lago de Freux
58 Festival de Agricultura
   de Libramont
59 Aldeia do Livro, Redu

Província de Namur
61 Paisagem com a Abadia de
   Maredsous
63 A Cidadela de Namur
64 Festival de Valónia,
   "les échasseurs"
65 Confluência do Sambre, um rio,
   e do Meuse, uma corrente
66 Produtos regionais
67 Vresse: o regato 'Calhaus brancos'
67 Fábrica de Cerveja de Abbey
   St.-Rémy
68 As Grutas de Han
68 Um Campo de Colza
69 A Cidadela e a igreja de
   Nossa Senhora, Dinant
70 O rochedo Bayard, Dinant
70 Morangos de Wépion
71 Os jardins de Annevoie
72 Descida de caiaque no Lesse
73 Carnaval em Vierves-sur-Viroin

Província de Hainaut
75 O Canal do Centro, A Louvière
77 A Grand-Place, Tournai
78 Belfry, torre de Tournai
78 Vista de Strépy-Thieu
   Ascensor de barco
79 Os 'Gilles de Binche'
80 Noite Musical de Beloeil
81 Igreja de Sainte-Waudru, Mons
82 Centro de Mons
83 Festival Doudou, 'Le Lumeçon'
84 Parque Pairi Daiza, Brugelette

84 | O Grand-Hornu
85 | Marsupilami, Charleroi
86 | Castelo de Seneffe
87 | Região das colinas
87 | 'Bois du Cazier', Marcinelle
88 | Castelo de Príncipes, Chimay
89 | O lago d'Eau d'Heure, Boussu-les-Walcourt

Flandres Ocidental
91 | O Mar do Norte
93 | Praça do Mercado com Tribunal de província e Belfry, Brugge
94 | Canais de Bruges
95 | Procissão do Sangue Santo, Brugge
96 | O porto de Zeebrugge
97 | Canal de Damme
97 | A Casa de James Ensor, Ostend
98 | Galerias Reais Leopoldo II, Ostend
99 | Porto Mercator em Ostend
100 | 'Het Zwin', reserva natural, Knokke
101 | Cabinas de praia, Knokke
102 | Camarões cinzentos flamengos
103 | Pescadores de camarões a cavalo, Oostduinkerke
104 | O Molhe de Blankenberge
105 | O 'Menenpoort' de Missing Monumento , Ieper
106 | A Beguinaria de Kortrijk
107 | Paragem de eléctrico em De Haan
108 | Lúpulo de Poperinge
109 | Windsurf, Mar do Norte

Província da Flandres Oriental
111 | Cais de ervas e cais de grãos, Ghent
113 | Adoração do Cordeiro Místico, irmãos van Eyck

114 | Azáleas de região de Ghent
115 | O Campanário, Ghent
116 | O'de Flandres, genebra da região
117 | Mercado de Flores, Ghent
118 | Castelo dos condes, Ghent
119 | Cuberdons, doce da região
120 | STAM: Museu da Cidade de Ghent
121 | Mola: Museu Provincial do Moinho, Wachtebeke
122 | Ghent: Área do Canal
123 | Estátua Mercator, Rupelmonde
124 | Mattentaarten de Geraardsbergen (bolo regional)
125 | A Koppenberg (colina), Oudenaarde
126 | CRVV: Centro 'Volta à Flandres em bicicleta' Museu, Oudenaarde
127 | Os pôlderes de St-Laureins
128 | Castelo de Ooidonk, Deinze
129 | Carnaval, Aalst

Província de Antuérpia
131 | Cidade junto ao rio Scheldt, Antuérpia
132 | Os 'Groenplaats' com a Catedral
133 | O Tribunal de Justiça
134 | MAS: Museu do Rio, Antuérpia
135 | O Mercado Grote, Praça do mercado, Antuérpia
136 | Viagem de barco Flandria, visita ao porto, Antuérpia
137 | Casa de Rubens, Museu, Antuérpia
138 | Museu do Diamante
139 | O Jardim Zoológico de Antuérpia
140 | Museu Plantin-Moretus, Antuérpia
141 | MoMu, Museu da Moda Antuérpia

142 | 'Kalmthoutse Heide', Reserva natural
143 | Klein-Willebroek
144 | Skywalk de Mechelen na Torre de St. Rombouts
145 | Catedral de St. Rombouts
146 | Bobbejaanland, Lichtaart
147 | Queijo da Abadia de Postel
148 | Zimmertoren (torre), Lier
149 | O Nete, Lier
150 | Filete de Antuérpia, produto regional
151 | O Castelo Bornem
152 | O 'Kabouterberg', Kasterlee
153 | Parque de Recreio Provincial Zilvermeer, Mol

Província de Limburgo
155 | Um pomar em flor, Haspengouw
157 | Colheita de maçãs, Haspengouw
158 | Tongeren
158 | O Parque Nacional Hoge Kempen
159 | Museu ao ar livre de Bokrijk
160 | Hasselt à noite
161 | Museu Nacional da Genebra, Hasselt
162 | As Grutas calcárias de Riemst
163 | Depósito de minério, Beringen
164 | Morcela, uma especialidade regional
165 | A região de Maasland
166 | Ténis, Kim Clijsters
167 | A região de Kempenland

ПОЯСНЕНИЯ К ИЛЛЮСТРАЦИЯМ MY BELGIUM

Брюссель – столичный регион
5 Гранд-Плас, рыночная площадь, Брюссель
6 «Маннекен Пис» («Писающий мальчик»), Брюссель
7 Бельгийский шоколад
8 Аркады в Парке Пятидесятилетия
9 Европейский Парламент
10 Королевские галереи Сен-Юбер
11 Мароллы, блошиный рынок
11 Уличные музыканты, Музей
12 Высокоскоростной поезд «Евростар» Брюссель-Южный
13 Парад Зиннеке, Брюссель
13 Музей музыкальных инструментов
14 Брюссельские вафли
14 Королевский театр Тоона (театр марионеток)
15 Королевский дворец в Брюсселе
16 Маршрут комиксов
16 Собор святых Михаила и Гудулы, Брюссель
17 Атомиум, Экспо 1958

Провинция Фламандский Брабант /Провинция Валлонский Брабант
19 Ландшафт между Дуйсбургом и Хульденбергом
20 Бегинаж, Дист
21 Муниципалитет Лёвена
22 Цикорий, местный продукт
23 Аббатство Авербод
24 Национальный ботанический сад
Замок Боухоут, Мейсе
25 Халлербос (лес), Халле

26 Соревнования по конкуру, Филипп Лежён
26 Музей сахара, Тинен
27 Гёз, региональный сорт пива
28 Суаньский лес, Тервюрен
29 Brussels Airlines, бельгийская национальная авиакомпания
30 День памяти в Ватерлоо
31 Холм Льва, Ватерлоо
32 Фонд Фолона, Ла-Юльп
33 Парк Сольвей, Замок Ла-Юльп
34 Музей Эрже, Лувен-ля-Нёв
35 Ландшафт Валлонского Брабанта

Провинция Льеж
37 Железнодорожный вокзал Льеж-Гийемен
39 Музей валлонской жизни
39 «Principautaires», Льеж
40 Собор святого Павла, Льеж
40 Фестиваль 15 августа
41 Дворец Принцев-Епископов, Льеж
42 «La Batte», блошиный рынок
42 Шахта в Блегни (уголь)
43 Льежские вафли
44 Окрестности Эвра
45 Валь-Сен-Ламбер, Серен
46 Замок Райхардштайн
46 Термы Спа
47 Гоночная трасса Спа-Франкошам

Провинция Люксембург
49 Могила великана, Ботассар
50 Аббатство Орваль
51 Заход солнца на фоне Церкви святого Мартина в Аарлоне

52 Базилика в г. Сен-Юбер
53 Река Семуа, Буйон
54 Крепость Буйон
55 «Jambon d'Ardenne», копченая ветчина, Сен-Юбер
56 Самый маленький город, Дюрбюи
57 Озеро Фрё
58 Сельскохозяйственный фестиваль в Либрамо
59 Книжная деревня, Реду

Провинция Намюр
61 Ландшафт с аббатством Маредсу
63 Цитадель Намюра
64 Валлонский фестиваль, «les échasseurs»
65 Слияние реки Самбры и канала Мёз
66 Региональные продукты
67 Вресс: бухта «blancs Cailloux»
67 Пивоварня аббатства Сен-Реми
68 Пещера Ан-сюр-Лес
68 Рапсовое поле
69 Цитадель и Церковь Девы Марии, Динан
70 Скала Баярд, Динан
70 Вепьонская клубника
71 Сады д'Анвуа
72 На байдарках по реке Лес
73 Карнавал в Вирв-сюр-Виройн

Провинция Эно
75 Центральный канал, Ла-Лувье
77 Гранд-Плас, Турне
78 Колокольня Турне
78 Вид с корабельного лифта Стрепи-Тье

79	«Gilles de Binche»
80	Музыкальная ночь в Белёй
81	Церковь Сен-Водрю, Монс
82	Центр Монса
83	Фестиваль Doudou, «Le Lumeçon»
84	Парк Pairi Daiza, Брюжлет
84	Гранд-Орню
85	Марсупилами, Шарлеруа
86	Замок Сенефф
87	Земля холмов
87	«Bois du Cazier», Марсинель
88	Замок Принцев, Шиме
89	озеро l'Eau d'Heure, Буссю-ле-Валькюр

Провинция Западная Фландрия
91	Северное море
93	Рыночная площадь с Епархиальным судом и колокольней, Брюгге
94	Каналы Брюгге
95	Процессия на празднике Пресвятой крови, Брюгге
96	Порт Зеебрюгге
97	Канал в Дамме
97	Дом Джеймса Энсора, Остенд
98	Королевские галереи Леопольда II, Остенд
99	Торговый порт в Остенде
100	Заповедник «Хет Цвин», Кнокке
101	Домики на пляже, Кнокке
102	Фламандские серые креветки
103	Ловцы креветок на лошадях, Остдюнкерк
104	Пирс Бланкенберге
105	«Menenpoort» Мемориала пропавшим без вести, Ипр
106	Бегинаж, Кортрийк

107	Трамвайная станция, Де Хаан
108	Хмель, Поперинге
109	Виндсерфинг, Северное море

Провинция Восточная Фландрия
111	Граслей и Коренлей, Гент
113	«Поклонение агнцу», братья ван Эйк
114	Азалии в окрестностях Гента
115	Колокольня, Гент
116	«O'de Flander», местный джин
117	Цветочный рынок, Гент
118	Графский замок, Гент
119	«Cuberdons», местные сладости
120	STAM: Городской музей Гента
121	Mola: Провинциальный музей мельниц, Вахтебеке
122	Гент: окрестности канала
123	Статуя Меркатора, Рупельмонд
124	Mattentaarten (местное печенье), Герардсберген
125	Коппенберг (холм), Ауденарде
126	CRVV: музей «Тур по Фландрии», Ауденарде
127	Польдеры Синт-Лаурайнс
128	Замок Ойдонк, Дейнзе
129	Карнавал, Аалст

Провинция Антверпен
131	Город на реке Шельда, Антверпен
132	«Groenplaats» с собором
133	Суды
134	MAS: Музей реки, Антверпен
135	Гроте Маркт, рыночная площадь, Антверпен
136	Прогулка на корабле по Фландрии, посещение порта, Антверпен

137	Дом-музей Рубенса, Антверпен
138	Музей бриллиантов
139	Антверпенский зоопарк
140	Музей Плантена-Моретуса, Антверпен
141	Музей моды MoMu, Антверпен
142	Заповедник «Калмтхаут»
143	Кляйн-Виллебрук
144	Смотровая площадка на башне Собора святого Ромбаута, Мехелен
145	Собор святого Ромбаута
146	Парк развлечений «Боббеяанланд», Лихтаарт
147	Сыр из аббатства Постель
148	Башня Зиммера, Лир
149	Река Нете, Лир
150	Филе по-антверпенски, местное блюдо
151	Замок Борнем
152	«Кабоутерберг», Кастерлее
153	Провинциальный парк отдыха Зилвермеер, Мол

Провинция Лимбург
155	Цветущий сад, Хаспенгоув
157	Урожай яблок, Хаспенгоув
158	Тонгерен
158	Национальный парк Хоге Кемпен
159	Музей под открытым небом Бокрейк
160	Хасселт ночью
161	Национальный музей джина, Хасселт
162	Известняковые пещеры Римста
163	Шахтный отвал, Берингген
164	Кровяная колбаска, местное блюдо
165	Регион Маасланд
166	Теннис, Ким Клийстерс
167	Регион Кемпенланд

LEGENDY MY BELGIUM

Bruksela – Region stolicy
5 Wielki Plac,
ulica Market Square, Bruksela
6 Manneken Pis (Siusiający
chłopiec), Bruksela
7 Belgijskie Czekoladki
8 Les Arcades du Cinquantenaire
9 Parlament Europejski
10 Pasaż św. Huberta
11 Marolles, pchli targ
11 Uliczni Muzykanci, Muzeum
12 Eurostar, szybka kolej
południowa część Brukseli
13 Zinneke Parade, Bruksela
13 Muzeum Instrumentów
Muzycznych
14 Wafle brukselskie
14 Królewski Teatr Toone (marionetek)
15 Pałac Królewski w Brukseli
16 Comic strip trail
16 Katedra św. Michała
i św. Guduli, Bruksela
17 Atomium, expo 1958

**Prowincja Flemish Brabant/
Prowincja Walloon Brabant**
19 Krajobraz pomiędzy
Duisburgiem a Huldenbergiem
20 Beginaż Diest
21 Town Hall w Leuven
22 Chicory, produkt regionalny
23 Opactwo Averbode
24 Krajowy Ogród Botaniczny
Zamek Bouchout w Meise
25 Hallerbos (las), Halle
26 Skoki, Philippe Lejeune
26 Muzeum Cukru, Tienen
27 Geuze, regionalne piwo
28 Las Sonian, Tervuren
29 Brukselskie Linie Lotnicze,
Belgijska Krajowa Linia Lotnicza

30 Dzień Pamięci w Waterloo
31 Pomnik Lion's Hillock, Waterloo
32 Galeria Folon Fondation,
La Hulpe
33 Park Solvay, Zamek La Hulpe
34 Muzeum Hergé, Louvain-la-Neuve
35 Krajobraz Walloon Brabant

Prowincja Liège
37 Liège-Guillemins Stacja kolejowa
39 Muzeum Walloon Life
39 "Principautaires", Liège
40 Katedra św. Pawła, Liège
40 Festiwal 15 sierpnia
41 Pałac Prince-Bishops, Liège
42 La Batte, pchli targ
42 Kopalnia Blegny (węgiel)
43 Wafle Liège
44 Land of Herve
45 Val-Saint-Lambert, Seraing
46 Zamek Reinhardstein
46 Termy Spa
47 Spa-Francorchamps,
tor wyścigowy

Prowincja Luksemburg
49 Wielki grobowiec, Botassart
50 Opactwo Orval
51 Zachód słońca za Kościołem
św. Marcina w Aarlon
52 Bazylika św. Huberta
53 Rzeka Semois, Bouillon
54 Zamek Obronny w Bouillon
55 'Jambon d'Ardenne',
wędzona szynka, św. Hubert
56 Najmniejsze miasteczko,
Durbuy
57 Jezioro Freux
58 Festiwal agrokulturalny
w Libramont
59 Book village, Redu

Prowincja Namur
61 Krajobraz z Opactwem
w Maredsous
63 Cytadela w Namur
64 Fête de la Wallonie,
les échasseurs
65 Zbieg Sambre, rzeki oraz
Meuse, potoku
66 Produkty regionalne
67 Vresse: Zatoka 'blancs,
Cailloux'
67 Browar Opactwa, St.-Rémy
68 Jaskinie Han
68 Pole rzepakowe
69 Cytadela i Kościół Naszej
Pani, Dinant
70 Skała Bayard rock, Dinant
70 Truskawki Wépion
71 Ogrody Annevoie
72 Wycieczka kajakowa, Lesse
73 Karnawał w Vierves-sur-Viroin

Prowincja Hainaut
75 Canal du Centre, La Louvière
77 Wielki Plac, Tournai
78 Wieża z dzwonnicą w Tournai
78 Widok z dźwigu Strépy-Thieu
79 'Gilles de Binche'
80 Noc musicalowa Beloeil
81 Kościół Sainte-Waudru, Mons
82 Centrum Mons
83 Festiwal Doudou, 'Le Lumeçon'
84 Park Pairi Daiza, Brugelette
84 Grand-Hornu
85 Marsupilami, Charleroi
86 Zamek Seneffe
87 Kraina wzgórz
87 'Bois du Cazier', Marcinelle
88 Zamek Książąt, Chimay
89 Jezioro l'Eau d'Heure,
Boussu-les-Walcourt

Prowincja Flandria Zachodnia
91 | Morze Północne
93 | Ulica Market Square z sądem wojewódzkim i dzwonnicą, Brugge
94 | Kanały Bruges
95 | Procesja Świętej Krwi, Brugge
96 | Port Zeebrugge
97 | Kanał Damme
97 | Dom Jamesa Ensora, Ostend
98 | Galerie Królewskie Leopolda II, Ostend
99 | Port Mercator w Ostend
100 | 'Het Zwin', rezerwat przyrody, Knokke
101 | Kabiny plażowe, Knokke
102 | Flamandzkie krewetki szare
103 | Poławiacze krewetek konno, Oostduinkerke
104 | Molo Blankenberge
105 | 'Menenpoort' Missing Memorial, Ieper
106 | Beginaż w Kortrijk
107 | Stacja tramwajowa w De Haan
108 | Chmiel z Poperinge
109 | Windsurfing, Morze Północne

Prowincja Flandria Wschodnia
111 | Graslei i Korenlei, Ghent
113 | Adoracja Mistycznego Baranka, bracia van Eyck
114 | Azalie w Ghent
115 | Dzwonnica, Ghent
116 | O'de Flander, regionalny gin
117 | Targ kwiatowy, Ghent
118 | Zamek Hrabiów, Ghent
119 | Cuberdons, regionalne słodycze
120 | STAM: Muzeum Miejskie Ghent
121 | Mola: Provincial Mill Museum, Wachtebeke
122 | Ghent: Kanał
123 | Pomnik merkatora, Rupelmonde

124 | Mattentaarten Geraardsbergen (regionalny wypiek)
125 | Koppenberg(wzgórze), Oudenaarde
126 | CRVV: Centrum 'Tour of Flanders' muzeum, Oudenaarde
127 | Poldery St-Laureins
128 | Zamek Ooidonk, Deinze
129 | Karnawał, Aalst

Prowincja Antwerpii
131 | Miasto wzdłuż rzeki Scheldt, Antwerpia
132 | "Groenplaats" z katedrą
133 | Sądy
134 | MAS: Muzeum przy rzece, Antwerpia
135 | Grote Markt, ulica Square Market, Antwerpia
136 | Flandryjska wycieczka łodzi, wizyta w porcie, Antwerpia
137 | Dom Rubensa, muzeum, Antwerpia
138 | Muzeum Diamentów
139 | Zoo w Antwerpii
140 | Muzeum Plantin-Moretus, Antwerpia
141 | MoMu, Muzeum Mody Antwerpia
142 | 'Kalmthoutse Heide', rezerwat przyrody
143 | Klein-Willebroek
144 | Most Mechelen na Wieży St. Rombouts
145 | Katedra St. Rombouts
146 | Bobbejaanland, Lichtaart
147 | Ser Opactwa Apostolskiego
148 | Zimmertoren(wieża), Lier
149 | Nete, Lier
150 | Filet d'Anvers, produkt regionalny

151 | Zamek Bornem
152 | 'Kabouterberg', Kasterlee
153 | Park rekreacyjny Zilvermeer, Mol

Prowincja Limburg
155 | Kwitnący sad, Haspengouw
157 | Zbiór jabłek, Haspengouw
158 | Tongeren
158 | Park Krajowy Hoge Kempen
159 | Muzeum pod gołym niebem Bokrijk
160 | Hasselt nocą
161 | „National Gin Museum", Hasselt
162 | Jaskinie marglowe Riemst
163 | Pozostałości kopalniane, Beringen
164 | Kaszanka, regionalny specjał
165 | Region Maasland
166 | Tenis, Kim Clijsters
167 | Region Kempenland

MY BELGIUM AÇIKLAMALARI

Brüksel Ba kent Bölgesi
5 Grand Place,
  Şehir meydanı, Brüksel
6 İşeyen Çocuk heykeli, Brüksel
7 Belçika çikolataları
8 Cinquantenaire kalıntıları
9 Avrupa Parlamentosu
10 St. Hubert Kraliyet Galerileri
11 Marolles, bit pazarı
11 Sokak Müzisyenleri,
12 Eurostar, yüksek hızlı tren
   Güney Brüksel
13 Zinneke Defilesi, Brüksel
13 Müzik Aletleri Müzesi
14 Brüksel waffleları
14 Toone Kraliyet Tiyatrosu
   (kuklalar)
15 Brüksel'in Kraliyet Sarayı
16 Çizgi roman yolu
16 St. Michael ve St.Gudula
   Katedrali, Brüksel
17 Atomium anıtı,
   expo 1958 Fuarı

**Brabant Flaman li /
Valon Brabant li**
19 Duisburg ve Huldenberg
   arasındaki manzara
20 Diest Beginaj Yapıları
21 Leuven Belediye Binası
22 Hindiba, bölgesel ürün
23 Averbode Manastırı
24 Ulusal Botanik Bahçesi
   Bouchout Kalesi, Meise
25 Hallerbos (orman), Halle
26 Binicilik, Philippe Lejeune
26 Şeker Müzesi, Tienen
27 Geuze, bölgesel bira
28 Sonian Ormanı, Tervuren
29 Brüksel Havayolları,
   Belçika ulusal havayolu

30 Waterloo'da Anma Günü
31 Aslan Tepesi, Waterloo
32 Folon Vakfı, La Hulpe
33 Solvay Parkı,
   La Hulpe Kalesi
34 Hergé Müzesi,
   Louvain-la-Neuve
35 Valon Brabant manzarası

Liège li
37 Liège-Guillemins
   tren istasyonu
39 Walloon Life Müzesi
39 "Principautaires", Liège
40 St. Paul Katedrali, Liège
40 15. Ağustos Festivali
41 Prens Bishops Sarayı, Liège
42 "La Batte", bit pazarı
42 Blegny Madeni (kömür)
43 Liège waffleları
44 Herve Bölgesi
45 Val Saint-Lambert, Seraing
46 Reinhardstein Kalesi
46 Spa Termal
47 Spa-Francorchamps,
   yarış pisti

Lüksemburg li
49 Dev Mezarı, Botassart
50 Orval Manastırı
51 Aarlon St.- Martin Kilisesi
   arkasından gün batımı
52 St.-Hubert Bazilikası
53 Semois Nehri, Bouillon
54 Restore edilmiş Bouillon Kalesi
55 'Jambon d'Ardenne',
   tütsülenmiş jambon, St.-Hubert
56 En küçük kasaba, Durbuy
57 Freux gölü
58 Libramont Tarım Festivali
59 Kitap Köyü, Redu

Namur li
61 Maredsous Manastırı
   ile manzara
63 Namur Hisarı
64 Wallonia Festivali,
   "les échasseurs"
65 Sambre Kavşağı,
   ırmak ve Meuse, akarsu
66 Bölgesel ürünler
67 Vresse: dere 'blancs Cailloux'
67 St.-Rémy Manastırı
   bira fabrikası
68 Han Mağarası
68 Bir kanola tarlası
69 Hisar ve Bizim Leydi
   Kilisesi, Dinant
70 Bayard Kayası, Dinant
70 Wépion çilekleri
71 Annevoie Bahçeleri
72 Lesse'de kano gezileri
73 Viervers-sur-Viroin'da karnaval

Hainaut li
75 Canal du Centre kanalı,
   La Louvière
77 Grand-Place, Tournai
78 Tournai çan kulesi
78 Strépy-Thieu gemi vincinden
   manzara
79 "Gilles de Binche"
80 Beloeil Muzik Gecesi
81 Sainte-Waudru Kilisesi,
   Mons
82 Mons merkezi
83 Doudou Festivali,
   "Le Lumeçon"
84 Pairi Daiza Parkı, Brugelette
84 Grand-Hornu Maden İşletmesi
85 Uzunkuyruk, Charleroi
86 Seneffe Kalesi
87 Tepeler bölgesi

87 | "Bois du Cazier", Marcinelle
88 | Prens Kalesi, Chimay
89 | l'Eau d'Heure Gölü, Boussu-les-Walcourt

Batı Flandre
91 | Kuzey Denizi
93 | Eyalet mahkemesi ve çan kulesiyle şehir meydanı, Brugge
94 | Bruges Kanalları
95 | Kutsal Kan Tören Alayı, Brugge
96 | Zeebrugge Limanı
97 | Damme Kanalı
97 | James Ensor Evi, Ostend
98 | Léopold II Kraliyet Galerileri, Ostend
99 | Ostend'in Mercator limanı
100 | "Het Zwin", doğa koruma alanı, Knokke
101 | Plaj kabinleri, Knokke
102 | Flemenk gri karidesleri
103 | Atlı karides avcıları, Oostduinkerke
104 | Blankenberge Rıhtımı
105 | "Menenpoort" kayıp anıtı, Ieper
106 | Kortrijk Beginaj Yapıları
107 | De Haan tramvay istasyonu
108 | Poperinge şerbetçi otları
109 | Rüzgar sörfü, Kuzey Denizi

Doğu Flandere
111 | Graslei ve Korenlei, Ghent
113 | Mistik Kuzunun Tapınması, van Eyck kardeşler
114 | Ghent bölgesinin açelyaları
115 | Çan kulesi, Ghent
116 | O'de Flander, bölgenin cini
117 | Çiçek pazarı, Ghent
118 | Counts Kalesi, Ghent
119 | Cuberdons, bölgenin tatlısı
120 | STAM: Ghent Şehir Müzesi

121 | Mola: Eyalet Değirmen Müzesi, Wachtebeke
122 | Ghent: Kanal bölgesi
123 | Mercator heykeli, Rupelmonde
124 | Geraardsbergen Mattentaarten (bölgesel kek)
125 | Koppenberg (tepe), Oudenaarde
126 | CRVV: Merkez "Flandere Turu" Müzesi, Oudenaarde
127 | St-Laureins polderleri
128 | Ooidonk Kalesi, Deinze
129 | Karnaval, Aalst

Antwerp li
131 | Scheldt nehri kıyısındaki şehir, Antwerp
132 | "Groenplaats" ile katedral
133 | Mahkemeler
134 | MAS: Nehirdeki müze, Antwerp
135 | Grote Markt, ehir meydanı, Antwerp
136 | Flandria gemi gezintisi, rıhtım ziyareti, Antwerp
137 | Rubens Evi, Müze, Antwerp
138 | Mücevher Müzesi
139 | Antwerp Hayvanat Bahçesi
140 | Plantin-Moretus Müzesi, Antwerp
141 | MoMu, Moda Müzesi, Antwerp
142 | "Kalmthoutse Heide", doğa koruma alanı
143 | Klein-Willebroek
144 | St. Rombouts kulesinde Mechelen gök geçidi
145 | St. Rombouts Katedrali
146 | Bobbejaanland, Lichtaart
147 | Postel Manastırı peyniri
148 | Zimmertoren(kule), Lier
149 | Nete nehri, Lier
150 | d'Anvers filetosu, bölgesel ürün

151 | Bornem Kalesi
152 | "Kabouterberg" Dağı, Kasterlee
153 | Eyalet Dinlenme Parkı Zilvermeer, Mol

Limburg li
155 | Çiçekleri açmış bir bahçe, Haspengouw
157 | Elma hasadı, Haspengouw
158 | Tongeren
158 | Hoge Kempen Ulusal Parkı
159 | Bokrijk Açık Hava Müzesi
160 | Gece Hasselt
161 | Ulusal Cin Müzesi, Hasselt
162 | Riemst kireçtaşı mağaraları
163 | Maden istifi, Beringen
164 | Domuz sosisi, bölgesel bir yemek
165 | Maasland bölgesi
166 | Tenis, Kim Clijsters
167 | Kempenland bölgesi

伝説

ブリュッセル - 首都地区
5 グランプラス、
 マーケット広場、ブリュッセル
6 小便小僧、ブリュッセル
7 ベルギーチョコレート
8 サンカントネール門
9 欧州議会
10 ロイヤルガルリ・サンチュベール
11 マロル地区、蚤の市
11 ミュージシャン・ストリート
12 ユーロスター、高速鉄道
 ブリュッセル - 南地区
13 ジンネケパレード、ブリュッセル
13 楽器博物館
14 ブリュッセル風ワッフル
14 ロイヤルシアター・トーヌ
 操り人形)
15 王宮
16 ミックストリップ・トレイル
16 サンミッシェル
 及びサンデュル大聖堂、ブリュッセル
17 アトミウム、1958 年エキスポ

**フランドル地方ブラバン/
ワロン地方ブラバン**
19 デュイスブルクと
 フルデンベルクの間に広がる景観
20 ディーストのベギン会修道院
21 ルーバン公会堂
22 チコリ、特産物
23 アーヴェルボーデ修道院
24 国立植物園
 ブショー城、メイゼ
25 ハラーボス（森）、ハレ
26 障害飛越、フィリップ・レジュン
26 砂糖博物館、ティーネン
27 グーズ、地ビール
28 フォレ・ド・ソワヌ、テルビュレン
29 ブリュッセル航空、
 ベルギー国営航空会社
30 ワーテルロー記念日

31 ライオン像の丘
 ワーテルロー
32 フォロン財団、ラ・ウルプ
33 ソルベイパーク、ラ・ウルペ城
34 エルジェ博物館、
 ルーヴァン・ラ・ヌーヴ
35 ブラバン・ワロンの景観

リエージュ地方
37 リエージュ - ギユマン
 鉄道駅
39 ワロン生活博物館
39 リエージュ
40 聖パウロ大聖堂
40 8 月 15 日祭
41 プリンス・ビショップ
 宮殿、リエージュ
42 蚤の市
42 ベルギー鉱山（石炭）
43 リエージュワッフル
44 エルヴ地方
45 ヴァル・サン・ランベール、セラン
46 ラインハルトシュタイン城
46 スパ温泉
47 スパ・フランコンシャン、
 サーキット

ルクセンブルグ地方
49 巨人の墓、ボタサール
50 オルヴァル修道院
51 夕日を背にした
 アーロンのサンマルタン教会
52 サンテューベルのバシリカ式教会
53 スモア川、ブイヨン
54 ブイヨンのフォートフィード城
55 スモークドハム、サンテューベル
56 世界で最小の町、デュルブイ
57 フルー湖
58 リブラモンの
 農業祭
59 本の村、ルデュ

ナミュール地方
61 マレツ修道院 の景観
63 ナミュール要塞
64 ワロニア祭り, les échasseurs
65 サンブル川と
 ミューズ川の合流点
66 当地特産品
67 ヴレス クリーク
67 サンルミー修道院の
 ビール醸造所
68 アン洞窟
68 菜種畑
69 要塞と聖母マリア教会、
 ディナン
70 バヤール岩 、ディナン
70 ヴェピオン産の苺
71 アンヌヴォア庭園
72 レスでのカヤック・トリップ
73 ヴィエルヴ・シュル・ヴィロアンの
 カーニバル

エノー地方
75 中央運河、ラ・ルビエール
77 グランプラス、トゥルネー
78 トゥルネーの鐘楼
78 ストレピ・ティウ船舶昇降機
 からの眺め
79 "Gilles de Binche"
80 ブロイユのミュージカルナイト
81 聖ウォードリュ教会、モンス
82 モンスセンター
83 ドゥドゥ祭り
84 動物園 、ブリュージュレット
84 グラン・オルニュ
85 マスピラミ、シャルルロワ
86 スネッフ城
87 丘陵地方
87 マルシネル
88 プリンセス城、シメイ
89 オードイル湖,
 ブッス・レ・ヴァルクール

西フランドル

- 91 北海
- 93 地方裁判所と鐘楼が建つ
  マーケット広場、ブルージュ
- 94 ブルージュ運河
- 95 聖血の行列、
  ブルージュ
- 96 ゼーブルッへ港
- 97 ダム運河
- 97 ジェイムズ・アンソールの家
  オーストエンデ
- 98 ロイヤルガルリ・レオポルド二世、
  オーストエンデ
- 99 オーストエンデのメルカトル港
- 100 自然保護区域、クノック
- 101 ビーチキャビン、クノック
- 102 フランドル・グレイ・シュリンプ
- 103 馬によるシュリンプ漁師
  オーストダインケルク
- 104 ブランケンベルグ埠頭
- 105 メニン門記念碑
  イーペル
- 106 コルトレイクのベギン会修道院
- 107 デ・ハーンのトラム駅
- 108 ポペリンゲのホップ
- 109 ウインドサーフィン、北海

東フランドル地方

- 111 グラスレイとコーレンレイ、ゲント
- 113 神秘の子羊の礼拝
  ファン・エイク兄弟
- 114 ゲント地区のツツジ
- 115 鐘楼、ゲント
- 116 地元東フランドル産ジン
- 117 花市場、ゲント
- 118 フランドル伯爵城、ゲント
- 119 キュベルドン、
  当地名物スィート
- 120 ゲント市立博物館、
- 121 地方製粉博物館 ワハテベーク
- 122 ゲント：運河地区

- 123 メルカトルの銅像
  ロベルモンデ
- 124 ゲラーツベーゲンのマッテンターアルト
  (名物お菓子)
- 125 コッペンベルグ（丘）、
  オーデナールデ
- 126 CRVV: "Tour of Flanders"
  センター
  博物館、オーデナールデ
- 127 ストラントーラン干拓地
- 128 オーエドンク城、ダインゼ
- 129 カーニバル、アールスト

アントワープ地方

- 131 スヘルデ川の町、
  アントワープ
- 132 大聖堂を伴う"Groenplaats"
- 133 裁判所
- 134 水際に建つ博物館
  アントワープ
- 135 グロート市場、
  マーケット広場、アントワープ
- 136 フランドリア・ボート・ツアー
  港周遊、アントワープ
- 137 ルーベンスの家、博物館、
  アントワープ
- 138 ダイヤモンド博物館
- 139 アントワープ動物園
- 140 プランタン モレトゥス博物館、
  アントワープ
- 141 MoMu、モード美術館
  アントワープ
- 142 自然保護区域
- 143 クライン・ウィッレブルーク
- 144 セントロンバウツ塔の
  メッヘレン空中連絡通路
- 145 セントロンバウツ大聖堂
- 146 ボッペジャーンランド、リヒタールト
- 147 ポステル修道院製チーズ
- 148 ジンメルの塔、リール
- 149 ネーテ川、リール

- 150 フィレ・ダンヴェルス、当地名物
- 151 ボルネム城
- 152 カステルレー
- 153 地方レクリエーション・パーク
  ジルフェルメール、モル

リンブルク地方

- 155 満開の果実園、
  ハスペンガウ
- 157 リンゴの収穫、ハスペンガウ
- 158 トンヘレン
- 158 ホゲ・ケンペン国立公園
- 159 ボクレイク野外博物館
- 160 ハッセルト・バイ・ナイト
- 161 国立ジン博物館、ハッセルト
- 162 リエムストの泥灰土洞窟
- 163 採掘集積場、ベリンゲン
- 164 ブラッド・ソーセージ
  当地スペシャリティー
- 165 マースランド地方
- 166 テニス、キム クライステル
- 167 ケンペンランド地方

图说我的比利时

布鲁塞尔 - 首都地区
5　大广场,
　　市场广场, 布鲁塞尔
6　小于连撒尿雕像, 布鲁塞尔
7　比利时巧克力
8　五十周年纪念门
9　欧洲议会
10　圣胡贝长廊
11　马洛雷斯跳蚤市场
11　街头音乐家,
12　欧洲之星高速列车,
　　布鲁塞尔南站
13　齐内克游行, 布鲁塞尔
13　乐器博物馆
14　布鲁塞尔窝夫
14　布鲁塞尔托内皇家剧院
　　（木偶）
15　布鲁塞尔皇宫
16　漫画步道
16　圣米歇尔及圣古都勒大教堂,
　　布鲁塞尔
17　原子球塔, 1958 年世博会

**弗莱芒-布拉班特省 /
瓦隆-布拉班特省**
19　杜伊尔赫和许尔登贝尔赫
　　之间的风景
20　迪斯特贝居安会院
21　鲁汶市政厅
22　菊苣根, 当地特产
23　埃雷伯德修道院
24　国家植物园
　　保朝城堡, 迈泽
25　哈勒博（森林）, 哈勒
26　场地障碑, 菲利普·勒热纳
26　糖博物馆, 蒂嫩
27　香槟啤酒, 当地特产啤酒
28　索尼恩森林, 特弗伦
29　布鲁塞尔航空公司,
　　比利时国家航空公司
30　滑铁卢纪念日

31　狮丘, 滑铁卢
32　弗龙基金会, 拉许尔普
33　索尔维公园
　　拉许尔普城堡
34　埃尔热博物馆,
　　新鲁汶
35　瓦隆-布拉班特省的风景

列日省
37　列日 - 吉耶曼
　　火车站
39　瓦隆生活风格博物馆
39　"市民"雕像, 列日
40　圣保罗大教堂, 列日
40　8月15日节日
41　王子主教宫殿, 列日
42　"巴特", 跳蚤市场
42　布勒尼矿山（煤）
43　列日窝夫
44　赫尔夫风景区
45　圣朗博, 瑟兰
46　雷因哈德斯汀城堡
46　斯帕的温泉
47　斯帕-弗朗科尔尚,
　　赛道

卢森堡省
49　巨人之墓, 波塔萨
50　黄金谷修道院
51　阿尔隆圣马丁教堂
　　后面的日落
52　圣胡贝教堂
53　瑟穆瓦河, 布永
54　布永城堡
55　"阿登火腿",
　　烟熏火腿, 圣胡贝
56　最小的小镇, 杜柏
57　弗瑞戴
58　利勃朗蒙特
　　农业节
59　书村, 雷迪

那慕尔省
61　马杜斯休养院风景
63　那慕尔城堡
64　瓦隆节, les échasseurs
65　桑布尔河和马斯河汇流之处
66　当地特产产品
67　夫雷斯: "白色鹅卵石"小溪
67　修道院酿酒厂
　　圣雷米
68　翰镇洞穴
68　油莱田
69　圣母城堡和教堂,
　　迪南
70　贝亚德岩石, 迪南
70　威朋的草莓
71　阿讷瓦花园
72　划皮艇游莱斯河
73　维耶尔沃叙尔维罗的
　　狂欢节

埃诺省
75　中央运河,
　　拉路维尔
77　大广场, 图尔奈
77　图尔奈钟楼
78　从斯特勒比蒂厄船舶升降机
　　眺望别处
79　班什狂欢节
80　伯勒伊音乐晚会
81　圣沃德吕修教堂, 蒙斯
82　蒙斯市中心
83　蒙斯杜杜节,
　　"鲁穆松"游戏
84　帕伊利戴扎公园
　　布吕热莱特
84　格朗奥尔纽
85　长尾马修, 沙勒罗瓦
86　塞内市城堡
87　丘陵地带
87　卡齐尔森林煤矿遗址
　　马西内勒

88 王子城堡，希迈
89 奥斯约尔湖，
布许莱瓦尔库尔

西弗兰德省

91 北海
93 市场广场、省级法院和钟楼，
布鲁日
94 布鲁日运河
95 圣血大游行，
布鲁日
96 泽布鲁日港
97 达姆运河
97 詹姆斯·恩索尔故居，奥斯坦德
98 利奥波德二世皇家画廊，
奥斯坦德
99 奥斯坦德的墨卡托港
100 茨温自然保护区，
克诺克
101 沙滩小屋，克诺克
102 弗莱芒灰色虾
103 骑马的捕虾渔民，
奥斯杜因坷克
104 布朗肯贝格码头
105 梅内恩失踪者纪念门，
伊佩尔
106 科特赖克贝居安会院
107 德翰电车站
108 波佩林赫酒花
109 风帆冲浪，北海

东弗兰德省

111 草巷和玉米巷，根特
113 神秘羔羊之祭拜，
凡·艾克兄弟
114 根特地区的杜鹃花
115 钟楼，根特
116 奥德弗兰德，当地的琴酒
117 花市，根特
118 伯爵城堡，根特
119 屈博东斯，当地的甜点

120 STAM: 根特市博物馆
121 Mola: 省级磨房博物馆，
瓦赫斯特贝克
122 根特：运河区
123 墨卡托雕像，鲁珀尔蒙德
124 赫拉尔德斯贝尔亨的马特蛋糕
（当地的糕点）
125 克朋贝格（山丘），
奥德纳尔德
126 CRVV: "弗兰德旅游"中心
博物馆，奥德纳尔德
127 圣劳仁的圩田
128 奥伊东克城堡，代因泽
129 狂欢节，阿尔斯特

安特卫普省

131 斯海尔德河畔市区，安特卫普
132 包括大教堂的"绿色城市"
133 法院
134 MAS: 河畔博物馆，
安特卫普
135 大市场，
市场广场，安特卫普
136 弗兰德利亚乘船游览
港口游览，
安特卫普
137 鲁本斯故居，博物馆，安特卫普
138 钻石博物馆
139 安特卫普动物园
140 普朗坦 - 莫雷图斯博物馆，
安特卫普
141 MoMu, 时装博物馆
安特卫普
142 "卡尔穆豪瑟草原"，
自然保护区
143 克基恩 - 威勒布吕克
144 梅赫伦圣罗穆博尔塔上的
天空步道
145 罗穆博茨大教堂
146 波贝杨兰德游乐场，
Lichtaart利赫塔特

147 波斯特尔修道院的奶酪
148 齐默尔塔，利尔
149 奈特河，利尔
150 安特卫普里脊肉，当地特产
151 波尔内穆城堡
152 "卡博特尔贝格"，卡斯特尔莱
153 省级游乐公园
齐维梅尔，墨尔

林堡省

155 鲜花盛开的果园，
哈斯蓬勾
157 苹果采收，哈斯蓬勾
158 通赫伦
158 霍姆凯姆普自然保护区
159 波克莱克露天博物馆
160 哈瑟尔特夜景
161 国家琴酒博物馆，哈瑟尔特
162 里姆斯特的马尔洞穴
163 采矿场，埃林亨
164 血肠，当地特产
165 马斯兰地区
166 网球，吉姆·克里斯特尔斯
167 凯姆蓬兰德地区

PICTURE RECORD/IMPRESSUM

Acke Patrick 10, 13r, 90-91, 97l, 98-101, 107, 109, 130-131 / Aerialmedia 70 l / Aerts Layla 145 / Antwerpen Toerisme & Congres 132, 135-141 / Antwerpen Toerisme & Congres en architect TV RRP/VK/OAP 133 / Blee Sarah – Neutelings Riedijk Architecten 134 / Brussels Airlines 29 / Centrum Ronde Van Vlaanderen: Demoor Marc 125-126 / Crab Jan 127-128 / Dani+1/2l / De Kievith 123r / Debeerst Philippe Photoeil 122 / Domein Bokrijk 159 / Eurostar 12 / Eye Flash 151 / Fédération du Tourisme de la Province du Hainaut: Carpentier C. 74-75, 78 l, 79-80, 83, 86-89 / Fototheek Scheldeland 129 / FTLB - Photo Willems Pascal 48 – 59 / FTPL - Gabriel Yves 39l, 42r – 46 l / FTPLimburg: America Annemie, Vaerewijck Michael 161 / Sweron Guida 164 / Wintmolders Kristien 154-155, 157, 158r, 163, 165, 167 / FTPN – namurclic: Bossiroy 63, 68l, 69, 70r / Genard Christian 60-61, 64-67, 68 r, 71-73 / OPT: Brancart Didier 30 / Claes Xavier- Soleil Rouge 35 / Remy J.P. 4 – 9, 11, 13l, 14 -17, 31 r – 33, 36, 39r – 42 l, 46r, 47, 77, 78r, 81 - 82, 84 – 85 / Remy J.P.- Atelier Port-zamparc 2009 34 /picture – alliance: 93 – 96, 97r, 103 – 106, 113, 166l / Provinciebestuur Oost-Vlaanderen 114, 116l, 121r / Provincie Vlaams-Brabant : Dewickere Stefan: 28l, Stad Gent – dienst Toerisme: 110-111, 115, 117-118, 120 / Streekproducten Vlaams-Brabant: Collet Luk 27 / Toerisme Hasselt: Vangelooven Philippe 160 / Toerisme Leuven 21 / Toerisme Limburg: 158l, 162 / Toerisme Mechelen: 144l / Toerisme Provincie Antwerpen: 142-143, 146, 148-149, 152-153 / Toerisme Vlaams-Brabant: 22 / Verhulst Dominic 18 – 19, 23 - 25, 29 / Loeckx Lander: 20r, 26 \ VLAM (VLaams centrum voor Agro- en visserij Marketing): 102, 108l, 119, 124, 150l / Vlegels Kris 147

1. Edition 2011

© Co-Copyright: Hallwag Kümmerly+Frey Ltd. Schönbühl-Berne, Switzerland. Daphne n.v. Gent, Belgium, www.daphne.be.

Concept / Editing: Caroline Acke, Lorenz Beer, Monika Petersen, Irena Senn
Design: Hallwag Kümmerly+Frey Ltd. / wa.zwei.werbeagentur
Translations: Caroline Acke, Consultra AG, Zurich
Image processing: Scanlith Ltd., Gümligen
Project- and Printmanagement: Media Impression, Switzerland
Overall production: Hallwag Kümmerly+Frey Ltd., CH-3322 Schönbühl-Berne
www.swisstravelcenter.ch

ISBN: 978-3-8283-0763-6